The characters and events portrayed in this book are fictitious. Any similarity to real persons, living or dead, is coincidental and not intended by the author.

ISBN-13: 9781969239021
ISBN-10: 1969239026

Cover and interior design by: ASH

OTHER BOOKS BY THE AUTHOR

A White Rabbit in Summer

Lovelife of a Deathdealer

Twisting The Turall

Ether

Voyage

Gold

Empathy

ROAD TO MALTHENA

and other poems

ASH

INTRODUCTION

Past the austere reflections, mixed into the idealism of catch all phrases meant to create the backbone of a better world, some true morsel of the human heart lied within poetry. It called to me from so far back I dared not remember my muse's shadow, but it was there. Lingering inside like the love that only hurts but none can avoid. I kept bumping against the edges of poetry confused, tinkering with it in the hope that it would somehow bolster my prose.

I'd heard many stories about how poetry moved someone. The way linguistic flourishes spoke to emotions beyond a dictionary, that love poem that made a cynic realize their contempt was birthed from a place of deep longing, that rallying cry that shifted shouts of malcontents into an anthem of rebellion, but that moment of inspiration eluded me. Best I ever felt was a smirk of appreciation for the horror in The Raven by a chamber door.

Ideas of Robert Frost's the Road Not Taken laid against defenses like some pillar against lumber protected mush. I thought only of all the regrets in my life, and nothing of the ABAAB meter that made each stanza complete.

And both that morning equally lay
In leaves no step had trodden black.
Oh, I kept the first for another day!
Yet knowing how way leads on to way,
I doubted if I should ever come back.

With time my wonder faltered, accepting that I would never feel poetry's allure. I was too dumb to compose on my own, too willful to repeat what works. I left all rythm to lyrics, singing only when the wind needed company. All my effort shifted to writing worlds of fantasy, talks of drama, and a fiction only my novels could produce.

But I was a diligent writer and in trying to hone my craft I came back to poetry time and again, writing over a hundred without zeal. Yet my love in the physical shook me out of my stupor, when their passion woke for haiku. They studied the art of short rhythmless meter, translated into excess by a tradition misunderstood.

I learned of a hermit named Nick Virgilio who spent his art writing three lines at a time. His dedication to editing was inspiring, and he supposedly spent many months perfecting this piece:

bass
picking bugs
off the moon

I saw what the work strove for and wondered why the image should mean more than the feelings they inspired. But another of Virgilio's works was striking and it broke through that prison of needing everyone to feel content:

the sack of kittens
sinking in the icy creek,
increases the cold

Natural physics teaches the opposite. The spread of life's end can only agitate the molecules into a negligible heat, but just as motion keeps water from freezing the sack of kittens would eventually leave no impact on the creek's temperature. What's striking about the poem for me is how observation is made into horror, speaking on the pragmatic desire to smother life before it can thrive the moment it becomes a nuisance.

And of course Virgilio's "the sack of kittens" speaks to me because of childhood robbed. The fact that it does with kittens has extra impact when cats shared my impoverish home.

Yet something else was shifting and had shifted in my mind for years. I was finally starting to see the utility of language, the way the parts of speech change meaning without changing a word. How a verb can be a noun and the reverse and how increases can be deceptively optimistic.

I was starting to see the beauty in language. I was learning how form could charm without function and felt a hunger for a driving beat. Through the works of Elizabeth Bishop I saw rhyme chains laid out like braids: each taking a turn to vanish in the same drama that great novels juggle plots. A favorite was the observational drama played out in "The Fish":

-- the frightening gills,
fresh and crisp with blood,
that can cut so badly --
I thought of the coarse white flesh
packed in like feathers,
the big bones and the little bones,
the dramatic reds and blacks

Seeing rhymes dropped early or slanted piqued my interest as poems never had. I could at last lose myself to sonic sensations echoed only in my mind. Thinking of meaning as I experienced instead of drawing them out in desperation. Reading poems finally brought a pleasure.

Another great change came as I looked for old works to favorite and new poets too obscure for their talent, I found my voice. And it came so swift that I was sure I'd faked it all and would lose it after a weekend with putting heart to pen, but it stayed. I switched styles, managed forms, and still it stayed. My voice, always too loud, and too insistent form an intense medium in the shortening format of poetry.

This book is composed of poems I wrote in 2024. I have divided the work up into seven categories for what I hope to be an ideal read. They are not in order of publication, but sorted by thematic direction. It was my intent for the poems to be read in order, but readers are invited to enjoy as they will. Some of my readers may even be familiar with my poetry. If so, I welcome your eyes and as always your feedback. Without your support, I never would've compiled this book.

My intent is for the poems to unfurl layers of artifice away as you read. I start with a collection of poems so abstracted that they are surreal or fantastical and then slowly come to bring you into my world, my mind, and finally my past before reaching the extended epic poem that is "Road to Malthena." A story of limerence and unrequited love, it is not a hero's journey, but rather the confessions of a villain. You may not like the person that I was in that poem and that's fine. I don't like him either, but he was who I needed to be to become something human.

Dissolved, surrealist poems not always direct.

Depressing, poems about the struggle of life, sometimes personal.

Defiant, a collection slam poems meant to scream against injustice.

Delusions, confessional poems that expose some of my ugliness.

The Map, poems about my past. This is the map leading to the Road.

Road to Malthena, lyrical poems all telling one story.

Dissection, a thorough look at how I constructed some of my poems.

TABLE OF CONTENTS

Dissolved

Depressed

Defiant

Delusional

The Map

Road to Malthena

Dissection

DISSOLVED

"Living On My Ceiling"

1
nowhere near enough were safe
when the world turned upside down
those walking and stuck in traffic
lost faster than any warning
2
I heard a call made it through
when the Earth shed its multitudes
there was too much wind to hear
what the people said on their descent
3
those at work survived for a time
but many more simply chose to join
the ever crystal blue that held aloft
every street, tower, and eyeball
4
falling furniture and priceless collections
preceded those hoping to reunite
with a world of graying skies and night
or simply to follow those that fell
5
in time we knew day was forever
the clouds had abandoned sky
as the sum of all discarded possessions
filled azure cracks like grout
6
now we who live on ceilings
know there is something there below
but for all of us who still think it up
we dare not risk that one-way trip
7
soon our food stores will spoil
now that global power has failed

we talk with shouts about the before
but do not risk a formal gathering
8
the last of the neighborhood dogs are silent
only birds add contrast to the screams
we sometimes convince the loudest to risk it
so that our ears can enjoy a reprieve
9
through the basement that was my attic
I've seen the empty rooms of neighbors
their whole life is now a humble reminder
that they too once walked on carpets
10
with every sleep expiration dates grow bigger
I ration by preservation but hunger for variety
my neighbors and I have all grown quiet
we're waiting to know that we're the last
11
I've found I don't spend much time walking
or even crawling up to the ground floor
my leisured default is laying by windows
waiting to see another bravely plummet
12
perhaps they've all found salvation
maybe I've failed this test of character
but I won't be fool enough to wager
that I am the last soul in my block
13
I remember a time when I went out
when dinners could be bought at a premium
but even that cost seems slim compared
to this world that knows no kilter

"Rainball"

Rain slides about that clear surface
implying a bowl beyond reach.
Under is dry but too haunting to sleep,
not even birds take sanctuary.
Supernatural novelty fades to small talk.

Taking out the trash; nervous.
The mistaken vessel is revealed whole.
A solid sphere of water, ripples,
elevating wonder to a text; that last friend.
Before motion ends, today calls.

At Monday's drudge,
in Friday's dazzle,
the water orb hovers.
Dust colors mud.
Passerines garden.
The suggestion of life
unfurls like ardent tea
viewed in still shot.

Curious but never forgot that ecosystem charms.
Weighed down by sediment the bottom hangs low,
low enough for a congregant to caress, but alarm
keeps even the selfies three respectful steps away.

Still, there is that one,
there is always them,
to walk that briskling path.

Catching fancies like honey,
gazes curving to windows
as envious hands anticipate
the moment the brave grows
close enough to drink shade.

Confident the elbow rises
uncertain the arm extends.
Not at the bottom but close
that one touches the surface.

Down comes the torrent,
mud, larvae, algae, and all
spreading over that courage.
The audience laughs
, rebuking their presumption,
confirming their impasse.
Comforted to remain dry.

But that one is more than wet
they are stricken by collapse.
For in that sphere's tumble
life is condensed flat.

Some are the eyes in comfort
and some walk in to touch
but all that witness magic
let art fade to small talk.

"daddy"

I don't know why, we call them spiders.

Those small things in webs
don't resemble the goliaths
whose legs are thicker than trees.

We can see their belly black
from below. It is featureless
and glossy and the women
wear nets after seasons rainy.
The elders say it is a web.
Cameras spotted their egg sacks
in the time of drones and bad facts.

Around us isn't dust, but the fibers of their silk,
the dangling horror of life turned to pellets.
Below the white-walk, in those holes where rain drops,
is the range of city stuff, read in the good-time books.
Back then a scream was honored and people ran to help.

So the elders say.

But I wonder
if any ever helped
except to watch
when they inevitably
were grabbed by fangs.

If one person out of a dozen
could shout loud enough
to leave a spider's prison.

If so I wanna go down and descend
to the place light has forgot.
I want to live in their schools
where cute boys wall slam me to flirt.
I want to watch life from phones

and laugh because danger is absurd.
I want to be anywhere but the safety
of the spider's curse.

Yet they are all around us.
In this world that has been lost
to the giants. And those who fought
died shouting for help,

begging for the multitudes
to come out of the shade
and assist in their death.

But I have never walked out into the direct light.
Nor has mother, for she values my life.
Together we follow this spider like a herd of
those *things*
I read in gentler times when heroes roamed.

Strange as it might sound,
I don't like the light hitting my ground.
The white-walk is safe.

Black legs a solid base,
when they move,
we run and as one body.
We starve no more.

"Party"

Alone in the boom, oriented by a flash.
Figures quiver from the veins of light's stain,
boxes, debris, a few coke cans, and one body.
Down on their side, remnants don't provide
a single clue to their physical status.

Without elec' apparatus,
can't tell what side is fucked,
only that this Hell is dangerous.
The gray might not fade
but a switch "on" means
I'm gone, cause these weekend
warriors have claimed the whole
quarter. Any sign of life, is a meal,
or a quick kill, a thrill to prop up
their balls like cialis after a night
of pick ups and vomit.
Going on this long mess,

my shoulders low, hiding 'neath the clock's hand.
I search a neck for a beat and only feel a cold grab.
This man's story's complete. His stubble a final clue
of his spent life. If he ever meets another coffin supreme,
they'll work his face clean for his interview with beyond.
And my mind's gone to be sharing this floor with a corpse,

but visibil' is a liabil' I can't afford.
Taking a stand will give me a target,
maybe that's how this man went
from kind and mellow to cold and hallowed.
I ain't hear no angel wings,
but the prayers sing loud enough
to hear the cries for Armageddon.
A society given up the fight.
Longing for our last rights,
until the day denied gives claim to demise.

It's me and that body hiding in this room. Outside they celebrate
the end of breathing. Jubilant crackles might shine this diamond
crazy, but this space has no way to save me from the mobs drunk
on hype. I purchased no guns but gained no license for peace.
My only hope of possession comes from my friend
lying dead on the eve of disintegration.

All the scared wallowers
are screaming with their souls.
When I close my eyes and listen,
ears go bloody. I'm cold.
With all the millions suffering,
silenced by a breeze,
started by scientists,
waving fans useless
on the embers of a dream.
Necks craned down forever
in a parody of respect,
the doom feeds curiosity,
turning parties circumspect.

So in my final moments,
watching skin turn to globs,
I reach up for my phone, and
willingly join our last mob.

"Mirthite"

Your laughter hangs in my room,
frozen by your sudden departure.

I suppose it's only fair to be gifted
such beautiful crystaline structures,
but spires of the lines slide off
anytime I review our last fight.

The last time I opened a window
wind disturbed their balance.
My memories left with the chill
and I'm paused at the threshold.

I can't get any work done when
I have to sneak in avoiding mirthite.
Perhaps the time will never be right
but I have to clear out the clutter.

It's time to break down your kindness
and sweep it all into buckets.
Every spindle and shaft of trust
needs to go out to the warmth.

I watch it melt to tears
and wonder when my warm cheeks
will feel the surface tension burst,
but I fear that too much of me is solid;
that my time of devotion was wasted.

What once could go out with trash
now must be emptied into the grass.
I hope the moisture isn't too salty
to grow amazing in your absence
but I know no seeds were planted
this garden of loss can only be weeds.

I miss how you laughed with me.

"on glass"

ghostly wind chills and sends cracks
through the scales of skin that rips
clean off in strips long and hard
by the subzero haunting white
that never fails to shred my

exterior

falls off like leaves on trees caught
up in some mythic deep freeze
flesh bared
bloodless from whispers
above and echoed down below

in silence

somehow one foot follows the next
creaking
my weak bones hunger for rest
on a tundra of time

lost to weakness
the forgotten still
humble my mind

how long before this
shell falls to fine
ribbon in cold mist

if you see me
weeping gently
don't come along yet
wait for sunset
when my bawling
feet are a wreck

if you hear me
walking shaky
don't call out yet
wait for regret
when my dying
heart
is circumspect

"The Company I Keep"

Death is a guest at my house. I can't say when
I invited her to stay, but she's always
around. She skips down the stairs and slaps
the ceiling, but I can't run with confidence when
my health is failing. She invites me to sleep when
the sun is high and wakes me from slumber

to spit in my eye. I know she's famous,
that the world delights at her dimples
and twirls, but I see her wrinkles
and converse, as her mannerisms
grow cold. Were I to shatter her dry exterior
I might find a solemn blaze sending smoke
to her every refrain. For there is a furnace in her cage
of ribs, and I saw her works melting within,

but a quiet guest proves a bad host.
She tires easily of the dreary and bores
of solitude. So I take her with me on rides
and she haunts my party nights.
She's always the life of the party,
no matter who wants her to be quiet.
I shouted at her for her behavior
but she was proud enough to deny it.

See, I was meant to serve her,
to entertain my guest of honor
and were it to rain
I should bend my back
to form an overpass.

This unsteady truce wasn't meant to last. The lady in her refinery expects a washroom full of glistening tiles and sharp surfaces. I can scrub to oblige, but lack the wits to serve a psychopomp. So in the light of a blinding cloudless morn, we paced about the room and argued about how I failed to show love. The dirty dishes that piled
were another sign of my neglect. I washed with frayed rags and she gave me a blade that I obeyed.

For three seconds I lived on that edge.

I felt every breath
and itched
at the murky dishwater
that clung to my skin.

I wanted to kiss her
and drink life's red,
but her kiss was all teeth
and her tongue was cold silver.

So we danced the pallbearer's gasp
until I was tired and she threatened
to buy new shoes, but all of my feet
were left and I had nothing

left to lose. In her boat
we traveled and through the mist
I saw running shades.
Below us my reflection
greeted me, but only rippled

when I waved. And out in front her lantern glimmered,
blinking hearts and horrors and night.
For there was another boat returning
and in its belly laid my gripes.

I woke to find her missing, but her cloak was sheered
and spread. Across every cushion and table, was a piece
that carried death. Between the threads, spiders
had crawled leaving silk

about the room. Following a dreary call, I walked through
the lines of doom and they clung to me like lace on
starlight. I dropped back to my comfort, sinking deep
into a coffin for three. There was plenty of room for all
of us, my heart, my hope, and she.

Now I dictate these words by ember,
in a house filled with mist.
My hosting skills have worsened,
but I can't get rid of my guest.
For she now owns my house keys
and she sleeps upon my bed
and once a memory it seems
Death invites company
to dine in my head.

"Sweet Teeth"

how long
must I feed you
past gongs
your midnight rings true
caressing prongs
catch skin and you
won't leave me to hemorrhage myself clean

in the sink
where I drip
all the cadence
I forget

convergence of moon and stars behind her black
wedding of ancient foes cervine and pack
mixing deadlines and wicked attacks
going til twisted joints break with snaps

how will the thrill dry on your gums

how long
must I feed you

effortless feast can't still taste so sweet

past gongs
your midnight rings true

must cavities be the thing that saves me

caressing prongs
catch skin and you

were I to rot my meat might claim you

all the rough ravage past savage divide
the hunger an ocean you swum to climb
and honest I go best when sails can rise
but lonely I know these tales won't suffice
when my beat sets meter of your meal tonight

oh sweet teeth
won't you leave me to hemorrhage myself clean

"No Lullabies"

enter storms naked
fell lilies on winter
be her shiny whore
his red satin cryptid

gather fallen stems
leave fowl for panther
cougar licks darling
smile to every friend

spirit bedroom eyes
oil up their spears
invest in fresh festoons
sleep with no lullabies

summer nights solace
blaze to melt hard butter
smoothly letters write
of sores left by promise

wash briny cobble
left white by surf
before shock blinding
lights text in rubble

love autumn morning
greet yesterday by hug
shiver not when solemn
twitch well with yearning

"Dark Comfort"

In all the darkness I fled,
it was within that comfort laid.
Eyes gently closed while held
in the embrace of an outsider.

Loki's kin, they was more beast
than friend. Even their smile, least
human. Pain was like breathing fast.
Loneliness reason to hold tighter.

Delighted by acceptance, unaware I was caught.
My every thrashing kindled a spark of lust.
Our bonding was scorned. Our candor, an ironic
disdain for order, natural or angelic.
Thus my escape would only give rise to mirth.

Alone on this Earth with a creature unwed,
they shattered my defenses with contradictions:
mine, not theirs. I was twisted; impaired.
Lost in cognitive challenge, my soul was laid bare,
or displayed on their table, a feast of raw passions.

My delectable flavor, left them oozing.
Sorrow was cloying, but gratitude filling.
I languished in hard haze, made tame
by consumption. A hard edge was left then,
a rage, shamefully fostered, betraying conscience.

I savaged and bit, fought snarling
beyond light's demand to be a star
I became the very pain I ought to deny.

My sacrilege, a demon's high.
All my fury, a welcomed treat.
They devoured all I gave and unsated,
pulled my sins out thread by morsel.
Ensorcelled by damnation's beauty,
left withered by my last strength's feat,
they had me dead to rights

and loved me forever instead.

"For His Eyes"

I wanted to lie with an angel
but received an honest kiss
an armful of feathers I hoarded

his year's molt my night's caress
in bliss I knew light's fantasy
but met his gaze before I finished

with scorn he watched me sin
but made no effort to join dark
begging forgiveness I stared and jerked
and not a feather upon him rose

perfect eyes damned me for wanting
yet his hard body remained til dawn

"Forest of Pain"

dry willow endeavor to go bald with dignity
shed threads grabbing paint from wonton wind
let arcs speak let motion outline brittle sallow
each crack bleats in harmony with hissing scald
washing wool in pots of stew mutton dying green
sitting butterfly below felled trees gone home again

tormented pine dine tonight in silence eyes turned low
past the growth lightning cracks the oldest embers glow
years abate making rings of gentle touch curving lifeline
shaping rage decorating campfire by their edge of light
all those words unspoken leave fuel for burning violence
electric shrieks of panic outside the attic exchanging blows
fist or tongue they batter dancing flames scatter over roads

where could the seeds escape
in the roar of breathing games
must every conflict echo late
rejoining ashes to fresh flames

with one sorry
pain
dissipates
but those
quarrels
end in rain

and saplings open

how ever fertile cruel ash might be
truth needn't burn false harmony
pruning words might cut too deep
but rotten cores are strong as ink
marking laws no culture keeps
for a forest floor no critter cleans
haphazard growth in sun that sneaks
through injured limbs loving carelessly

kissed
in
smoke
skies
youth
finds
time
to climb
the rays

rejoice as they join
the forest of pain

"U t7t d P4art"

a)beit in sm
ways I kn
zt my Ery
prot(station s not)ng
m+
zan ze
faffng abt
f a looooo0000000zer
who s made
np coolR
by ze ver con(nected exp)eriment...s
f ballista thrown
fast by
<{[(unseen trebuchets)]}> made 10ade ^on |c|uries
past thro
wing sto
)nes far in2 ze future 2
destroy ~castles bt homes
which will soon b ze wandRng
automachines
that we (bleed
desert livs
2 fit -V- our contra)
ptions in n as L o n g
as we're on ze
subject cn sm1 pls
object 2 ze idea
zat o(U)r lived area^2
need b a plot
of land
zat
cn
b
purch(a$$$$)d

when o(U)r $Rvice 2 zis country ought 2
demand smzng   more   zan   debt
n
shell shock
yet sooooooooooooOOOOOOOOOOOOo m+y
vetRans
receive the
quality f
paper[_]s   left 2 rot in
c o r n e r s
zat sag from the w_e_i_ght f
unprocessed requests
bc ze $taff s _R$taffed inten?onally s,o
zat zese de*cora*ted heroe$ cn -V- decay
2 zero
w ~chance f R+ry bc we've built a   so-sOO-society
2 punish
anyzng
zat req $ while still $pending
ze bulk of o(U)r $undng
on ze war machine
zat consumes   -V- genius
wh!e
givng   back
~$timulu$ 2 the sm livs zat need .

"We Name Them Murder"

crows speak with intonation and frequency
crows think but don't seem to count past six
crows debate with the insistence of children
crows fight to make themselves difficult targets
crows understand consequence and buoyancy
crows congregate for reasons only known to the

murder

fours and sixes and groups of more
may speckle dimming blue skies
but they do this with a rarity
that suggests that their gathering
is done with an intentional profundity

when do these daytime journeys become murders
when are their discussions meetings of state
when does their silence mean
more than to announce one's presence

every murder has its mystery
every scholar has their theory
every summer has a blistering

heat and should that be avoided
autumn will correct its absence
like an abscess allowed to breathe

no matter the mess
no matter the dead
crows will fly in
abundance to clean

and we the great
disruptors resent
how they remind us
how crows are in need

"stubborn vine"

Unwelcomed, vine climbs against a creek who won't speak. Sentimental brook babbles to rocks of channels neither had seen. Yet stone and drip both give in to a curiosity and think about that misinformed ivy. Submerged by strange purpose.

Still green. Still okay.
Leaves grow out but under
that rushing water;
moving too slow to bother
chatting with that slithering.

Out
peaks one leaf.
Climbing sheet

tenderly approaches sky that calms and sighs and gives no goodbyes through hateful summers but already the chlorophyll fails. One timid greeting ends in a crinkling twilight. Clouds darken somber to begin an acupuncture of piercing hail.

Still twisting. Still alive.
Warm sun will come again.
Fast water, furious, subsides.
Back to chill fête with smooth
companions and that ivy

breaks free of the surface tension! In that light of refreshing shine, doth nourishes young hopeful vine! The worst burden shed like dew drops on a sweet tongue past morning's rise. It climbs! So brilliant and alive that all of nature gasps and stirs sublime.

Here comes a victory worth the bluebird's time. He soars arcing interested in the lively thrive. One leaf comes out thicker and bold curling to form a line. That raucous bachelor takes a perch and sings to good minds and warm nests. Let the best feather breasted

mother gather twigs and support this vine. All the creatures loud and small, came to gaze as that space was filled up full. Through a life green and wonderful, a community formed around that miracle.

Yet no trumpets sound to celebrate that climb.
Instead gray comes to dominate the sky.
Still that yellow striped warrior survives.
Amongst doubting creek and oriole speak
the eyes all look on curiously
as splitting vines fall ominously
back to waters taking detritus downstream.

Hark, that light again! A brilliant accompaniment, to that stubborn glorious vine, that had already shook the worst and darkest night. For the first time that climb won't follow a beam up high. It's twisting form went inward, wrapping branches inside edges,

a leg takes shape and steps upon the creek.
A human frame wrapped sinuously
to make an arm raised valiantly,
but the body stops short of chest.
The rest did it's best, but were only vines.

Reaching inside,
it comes for the couple. Mother and father guard
their quintuplets. Giving a flight, they scratch,
peck and bite. The injustice and spite!
What once was a home, the human
now comes for their kin.
Taking the nest firm, it yanks life out from it.
Crushing the eggs,
a wind blows with violence.
Every leaf and twig, withers and dies instantly.
The great opposition to life
now falls to pieces in the stream.

Still the creek
and the rocks
they talk.

stubborn vine DX???

I wrote three versions of this poem: "stubborn vine", "starless vine", and "surviving vine" make up my vine trilogy. You can see my thoughts on these poems on page 256.

"surviving vine"

unwelcomed vine climbs against a creek
brook babbles derisively
yet out from the water
a lone leaf peaks out farther
sun nourishes green tenderly
but that leaf can't leave the drink

it crumbles brown
and goes downstream
a shivering sky
cries hail for thee

past the mourning
sun brings a fresh attempt
in one burst the ivy
rises past surface tension

against all nature
that vertical vine
brings a joyous bluebird
he takes a perch
and sings of new birth
a lady comes to build a nest
supporting ivy with the rest
a hundred critters give their time

yet from up on high
there isn't a faint sign
of support just the pour
of darkness and cruel time

but as Earth spins round
the vine it found
a reason to thrive
more than the day it survives
the ivy resembles human life
a leg a body with an arm

that stops short of chest
the vines all did their best

reaching for the nest
the birds take the fight
they harry harsh plant
but can't stop the vines
that nest comes out fine
but in a hand of ages
it crushes five young eggs
the wind blows with violence
every leaf dies instantly
that great opposition to life
falls to pieces in the stream

brook babbles derisively

"Under Yggdrasil"

Still
pond under Yggdrasil.
Kissed.
Cherish
last drop.
Scorch
my
drink.
Steam
walk
root
and
bark.
Branches
branch
and split
again
every path
sturdy as the next.
fight fledg l in g b ir d s
for hole
they fall to ground
I sleep sound.
Night
takes my mind
but gives no
r e s t.
Tested and failed
Wake with dew and drop
into
my lips
sucking
crisp
life.

"Confrontation"

I fell asleep reading poetry on a reviving
summer day. The poet was before me,
in an indoor basketball court in the inner

city. He stood resolute like granite
and his sides were chipped to shale.
There was no impact he didn't own,
no misery he tried to hide.

My scorned thoughts brought him forward,
my critiques his calling card. With the temperance
of a soldier, he demanded I be honest
with my scars. Though he was small

and I larger, I was certain my advantage
would hold. Should a fight break out
between us, my skill would render him
on the floor.

But those around us knew his face
and through his work, his pain,
and I was a loud-mouthed foreigner,
a tourist with a notepad.

No force of blows would win this,
no confrontation would end as mine.
He'd already lived at least four lives
and had the support to live nine.

So I had no choice to be honest and I'm too weak
to speak with pride. So I told him his work

made me angry and brought no tears to my eye.
His rejection of form broiled me, it left me bitter to see
him hide, the pain that obvious in him when I looked
in those dark eyes. For when I bleed,
I bleed in earnest,
I've no valve to twist,
no mask to hide.
And all his poetic implications meant
only those closest could look inside.

He could've laughed,
he could've walked away,
he could've sent his fans to break me.

Instead, he passed a ball
and told me to shoot.
I said I couldn't pay anything if I missed.

I expected the aphorism about missing

shots never took, but he said

poems are like basketball where the court's invisible.
You only play against yourself and your success is on the replay.
There you'll hear the whole crowd cheer
and witness the scoreboard light.

I hated his analogy and was angry

that art needed spectators to be just. He said,
"Relax, don't worry."
and faded into dust.

The court was all but empty,
the hoops present with the lines.
But with no one around to see me
all I could do was practice.

I wonder what he'd do if
I spoke my anger to his face.
But knowing him, I wouldn't be there,
he's protected by his fame.

Yet in an artist's work they're copied.
His vision representing his heart's blood.
So if I dreamed that encounter,
maybe the poet and I talked.

"Atrophied Wings"

We need to acknowledge the atrophy of wings.
Edicts complacent keep our sore feet on concrete
but between the pushing of pedals and poking black cells
we work knees, unlatch window panes, and fly.

The soaring is spectacular, the displays hydrate
my dry horrendous spine like rain on crags.
That motion bold towards endless, brings tears
to my sighs, and every aerial flourish does galvanize
my overwrought conviction to join that brilliant climb.

Sadly, we are not even geese in spring.
Our shoulders overburdened by compulsory OT.
We go not gently, but we can't wait for night.
Migration requires fattening, but our obesity
weighs down beating valves and no salve
saves a lonely couch with a tumor of our hide.

Soar,
if that aching cartilage won't bend.
Jump,
when you're too low to descend.
Run,
to get that lift under your hope.
Crawl,
despite all that tonnage of woe.

Shake free this atrophy
and fly to every sky.
Keep high in symphony,
speak the anthem inside.

"without scabs"

up rolls the blood back to the hurt
crimson rain there again domed with tension
sinking into crevices a fissure once shook

shatter clicks and clatters from wall to cup
twirling ever tight to center finding focus
a liquid clear as insults spinning tilted half full

goblin in a hobbling dip cheers to raise an arm
that snarling grin comes to an end
as the cup recovered by gentle palm

that red and green monster settles into motion
creaking down like timber sawed his knees
crashing like a sheet snapped tight on the breeze
what was horrible is now more of a guest
than a pest that can't be suffered to live

and the blood was never there
it was a fantasy
why would anyone care
about the ramblings
of some bag of strings

tied so tight
that none can tell
where its mouth and its tail
are separate

so just forget

about the cup

cause the glass
was never empty
it was always
going to be the last
reason for suffering

and the ring is nothing
more than a marker upon that saucer
like the threshold of a door
once closed aught be ignored
so don't start thinking
that men are evil
when that fine guest
was nothing short of the sort
of friend that people need

none aught to turn away good company
sitting in corners brings monotony
to revelatory praise of indolence

that man rises up from that seat and that cup
that wasn't filled but never empty on that surface
that should be scrubbed clean before he got here

and foot falls sound his exit or maybe follow his entrance
a rap of knuckle to sliced tree brings eyes to a pouring stream
cold pitcher of his water filled wrong for gentle father

DEPRESSED

"starless vine"

I see you.

Climbing against the current,
you grow like ivy
and you've earned it.
Don't let them freak you.

They want a feast to go with their show,
ignore them all continue to grow
up to that light.
Your first shimmer of soul
might not survive a night,
it could wither at the first exposure.
Don't let that feeling own you.

Ignore the doubters outside and within,
begin to trust that thrust for life.
Your soul will shine,
let it be bright!
You'll know you've made it
when you rise up against the stream
to take shape independently.
And the praise will come
and it'll come loud
and you'll inspire others
and feel proud
to watch their success
and know their growth
and you'll breathe hope.

And yet I see you

I see you thrashed by every laugh
and curl up and hide your light.
You could stand tall, you could be bold,
but every setback becomes a goal
of nothing or it all. And when you stumble,
you think it's a fall.
And the thing that gave you joy
causes pain and so you destroy
that very thing
that you came to live for
and what was inside
dies.

When you take it all
you don't leave anything
for the fall.
I wished you'd look past night,
to see the brilliant starlight.

"Silver Revelry"

Fire the governor.
Their absence opens the sky.
It's fun to watch a city burn
but harder to live in ruin
while smoke reds the eye.

But those tears seduce, polymorph loneliness into a haunted lament. A scream, night scare, the living scene of reality partitioned to your playground. Becoming the butchered muse and mutilated artist both to savor the drama. Every line of thought, silver. Moon kissed weaving to cement your ascent, but razor thin cuts prove your web is the pup'teer's performance. You, the doll to your unbridled mare, nighting your race to a fall.

Reclaiming midnight one bellowed "fuck" at a time.
Coffee or gin, you've chosen your tonic,
to stave off sleep with a crafter's need.
Unlocked and worn wild, past smiles,
past dread, past all the fuckers still
yammering in your head. Undead,
but unrequited, no quieting comes
from the paint splatter or groans.

A toilet bowl dyed by your veins.
A crow's claw fraying the lens.
A rooster caw begging the end
of insomnia, but sun colors your shades.
There's no grave til the fae shake
is honored in full glorious quake
of your soul long since denied
the healthy outlet you once liked.

But the choice for a mind freed
smothered every pragmatic bent.
Your last rational choice spent

on sustaining a season of infestation,
the pest, your very own drive to be more
than that worthless bore you observe
in the mirror. Pain has taken over
where preservation once implored
you to brush teeth and talk clean.

Now a zombie, your mind an echo
of the person your once despised.
Loved ones realize your spark
has been given to years of art.
And though your soul was manifest
all minds are too busy to bear witness.

Heed this warning,
of the muse's allure.
She will kiss your heart electric
but fuck your life bare.
In her one tiny outlet,
you may scream for help
but loud as you shout it,
you will collect dust on a shelf.

"Bad Weaving"

weaving art from dreams
insomnia threading string
expelling passions depart
leaving eyes dry, head numb
tired from heart's extremes

guilty like a lush wet from a fling
flattery took over, I succumbed
to a muse's playful gleam

brushing off yesterday's bad
a walk of shame fit for a King
fingers a comb for greasy coif
I take my role as one colonnade
supporting a structure in my stand

natural gazes redden cheeks to blush
scoff at innuendos in a telling way
until all assume my secret shame

bad yesterdays off brushing
dreams from art weaving

Bad Weaving DX???

This poem has had a more thorough dissection where I break down the form and intent behind the poem. You can find this dissection on page 242.

"About That Ruckus"

I screamed so loud my ears hurt
with a frequency that strained
my voice back to a whisper
when I was finally heard I burned
held over the cleansing flames
of propriety that reminded me

there is nothing noble
about dying in public
my end must come in secret

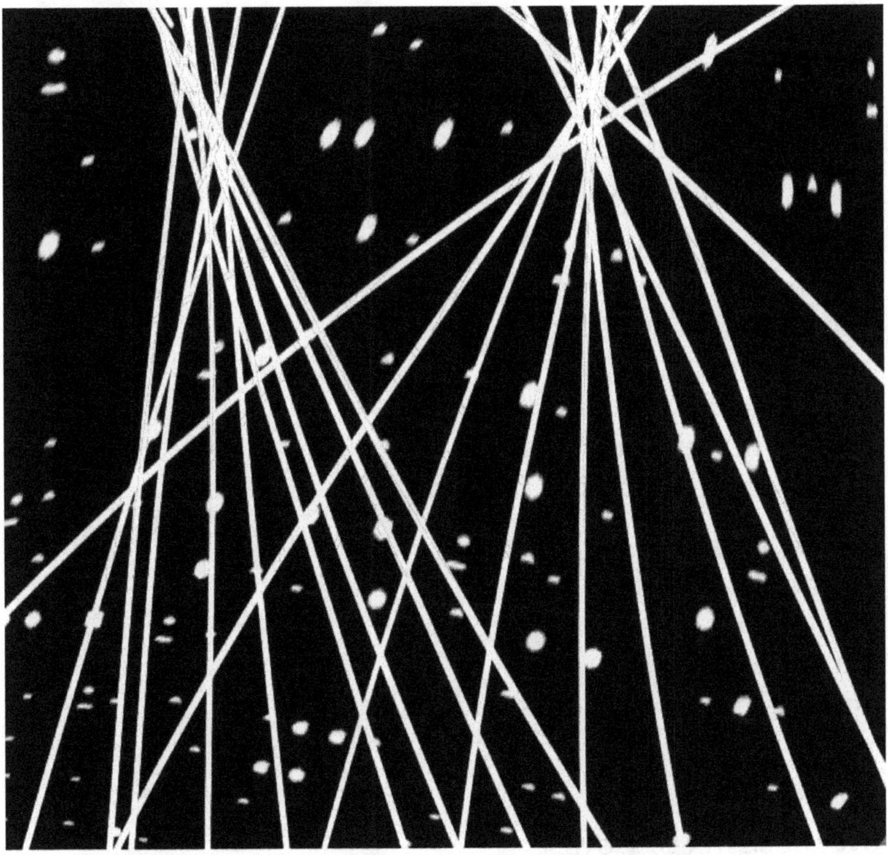

"Jet Ski"

The soundscape
of your life take,
sent me surfing along on the ripples
turned to dreamwaves.
I was jet skiing through it all.

Though I've never
quite felt it,
the rush and sick jump
seem like something big.
Your brain can't be spilled in an afternoon's tea.

So join me
in misty buoyancy.
Navigating the crash of global gravity,
that cloying culture sputters me.
Will you be there when my engine hacks?

I've tried to crash through it all.
Cutting waves and steering tall,
but my gut gets mashed
and tenderized. In your eyes,
I see the answers I seek
give me the question to speak
only share more from your candid side.

I need direction,
something spiritual,
and you've never been a prophet
but a friend replied,
and I need bright wisdom tonight.

All my lonely
evenings fretting
over hope freezing over
by degrees. My sanity
is creaking to that point of split.

This is it.
All my time,
spent considering my whole life
like film losing fidelity.
I've run out of road to flee.

I'm ready to jump; no wings!
You've got me thinking of flight
making real twilight
from dreams lost to apnea.
There'll be a road to swim back,
when the motor grimly hacks
it's final breath, built by your axioms.

As the moon
shines on the water
that new path
takes me further
to some good at last.
Gimme just one
word to live for.

"With Apologies"

I will never forgive
myself for participating
in my own abuse
why should you

my loneliness
is what I deserve
my every suffering
earned

I understand why I must hide
the self hatred inside
we are all fighting
that monster
and so to see my sorrow
is to feel that echo

with apologies
I'll silence
what's bothering me

so that you might
smile before
the blood dries

"A Child's Fairytale"

Once upon a lie
her gloved hand in mine
a tandem turn as we glide
composed and keeping time

I lay down steps like a rhyme
making me worthy to find
her crimson lips spreading wide
to tell me I'm welcome inside

her heart's chamber divine
so that I might savor sublime
that carnal hunger that thrives
despite all temperance outside

A Child's Fairytale DX???

This poem has had a more thorough dissection where I peel back some of the language and explain my intent for this poem. You can find this dissection on page 271.

"Margarita"

Ever sweet **Margarita** *how we adore your style*
You flit about the room beguiling
escorted to many flings

Always kind **Margarita** *you grace us with your smile*
Your effervescent charm is effortless
suggestive pauses that loosen lips

Fine and alluring **Margarita** *why must your kiss be sour*
Your stalwart grit demands our savoring lick
yet chills our yearning thick

Aloof and cruel **Margarita** *why can't you stay an hour*
Your fully packed schedule leaves us breathless
when flirts cut a deep jealous

Delightful and dangerous **Margarita** *we crave your citrus dance*
Your presence surpasses luxurious appraisal
on or off our table

Agave tongued **Margarita** *won't you give us the chance*
You can't expect an early departure
must we pay to keep your ardor

Fickle ruinous **Margarita** *we cherish your every caress*
You fill our nights with victories and regret
no matter how many we forget

Twisted haunting **Margarita** *won't you give us solemn rest*
Your grudge sickens and grips our throats
hazy eyes and glass shattered roads

"Distraction"

coke drips
from a tab
on a can
in a cup
on a desk
by the mess
where letters
and notes
suck thoughts
from my head
meant to write
but I can't
since I lack
will to grab
the trash
and stash
in a bag
clearing desk
to discover
the next
excuse

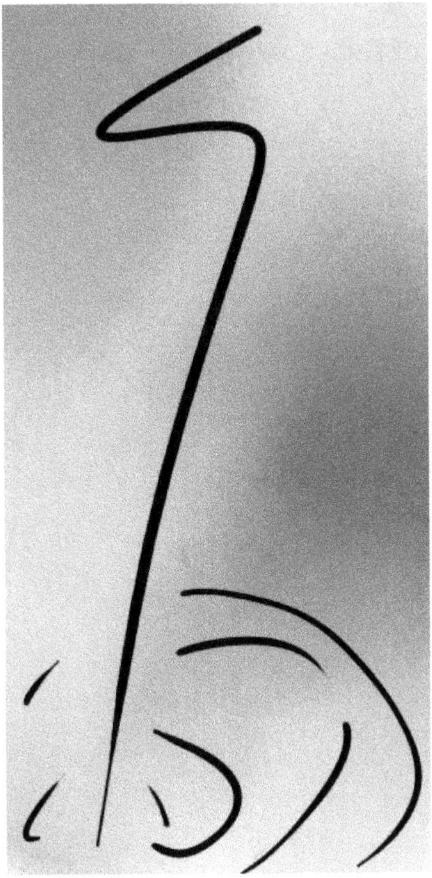

"Piercing Charity"

the saddest thing is kindness
genuine and without expectation
its rarity penetrating layers of cynicism
hemorrhaging heart's feel total
plasma and red exposing what's dear

and in that pain of surprise
we are touched and seen
our edges suddenly solid
crying with gratitude
fearing coagulation
will bring our beat
back to the stillness

of the grave

"a wish"

I'll read your poem.

You'll perform mine.
Wrapped in your blanket.
You'll laugh.
I'll cry.

Why couldn't I say goodbye.

"Secondhand Damnation"

gripping tar slipping shards a blade below the stucco
breathing parts boiled dark from a brew tobacco
inward curls fingers seasoned sticky with smoke
raucous shore line deepened by grasping my throat

heaven knows that angels aren't composed of gray
but the fade of want endless drifts by hurricane
wings silent hovering on splintered homestead
septimal gems eye prayers answered with death
each pair a promise to those of faith unbent
the last a beacon leading fog-lost to debt-worn graves
my feet hover as firm hands purple my malaise

round
round
we lilt level with ground

tilted
jilted
my ange' soothe mewling sound

somber
gentle
my soul flitters half down

whilst
wing
beats
off vital pulses around

and
about
my neck

for that
tar
cloys
my sense

a child that wants horrors I had noticed
but never worried that shades hungered
after lungs were chewed to shreds
that passing moment of strangers enjoying
the third half broken dark and chewing
long and joyous and stretched to touch my scent

let that seraphim douse
every whim in a bath
I can't remember
her lies came with my cries of salvation
bought in shame's anger
so let heaven's resuscitation
come on lips wide and patient
and through a ghost's kiss
give that gift of life smothering gray hurt

Secondhand Damnation DX???

This poem has had a more thorough dissection where I try to explain some of my intent for this poem, focusing on the symbolic. You can find this dissection on page 272.

"To The Silent Readers"

don't like or vote or comment
know that your silence is gold
your presence isn't always safe
they lie to welcome all with grace
smiles and best wishes will fade
warm bonds include a few
there's no way to make that you

stay a lurker
watch them move
by their shadows

DEFIANT

"To Those Born Earlier"

you spoke of hatred's slumber
of inequality's end
applause boomed like thunder
you were heroes of your day
yet every year and more thereafter
laughter joins the pain
because rebellion of sin is sentimental
but it's coopted all the same

kids are trained in your foul swamps
their small forces make a heroic stand
for sixty dollars every Christmas
we relive your deaths by shouting match
you passed your days in fear and hunger
we pass our time congratulating chat
and should snooty artists criticize the game
political motives can't live in Nazi hats

my parents suffered your distorted features
and still cower from your raised voices
every year your struggle seems less distant
as politicians direct fear to make a sequel
I know their deaths took their toll
that the blood would never rinse
but when you brought home toughness
did you have to neglect our education
we needed not the experience
of glory bought with a-bombs
but the eyes that witnessed injustice
and the ears that learned fascist songs

did you not trust us to share empathy
to give the purple hearts a mend
did you have to luxuriate in amnesia
bought with alcohol shaped by grit
couldn't you have at last given voice

to the injustice before you
instead of beating our parents
so low that they spoke of peace
as police tested the tensile strength
of bone did your home have to feature
in the prison that you engineered

must the sins of our fathers blind us
to the rise of home grown despots
that this fresh ilk of racial supremacism
were trained to kill by playing your wins
must our still beating hearts bleed
until we all have grown so wild
that a new generation lacks human beings
and that animal within is a specter
of better times as it gave us no will to survive
but a fury to bite hands that feed and embrace
and a rage that burns hotter than sense
must we relearn to bury bodies a hundred deep

and you ask us for leniency???

I have no spiritual indulgence to sell
I lack the mind space to spare pity
to the generation that shaped
the way we process a massacre
you had it all and you bought relief
now we sell liberty
and as you know
it comes cheap

"Guns Without Ammo"

did he save our country
did he spread our fear
did he shape our unity
or merely hide tears?

he is a plaster thin smile
he is a thousand mile stare
he is still stiff at attention
and fighting everywhere

yet the battle never won
wasn't meant to be a bottle
prescription or glass
it speeds the years past
ever closer to that closer
a crash of metal full throttle

denied by fate
twisted by lies
robbed by congress
selling what's inside

and there's not much left
for the guns without ammo
if they saved any bullets
it's for their final salvo

and the good ones
died young
so the live ones
ain't sung

every monument
to mass death
a reminder that next
is too far and too many
and the gone

never left pretty

so to live on
honors every scar
but the give is beyond
what any man has
with the toll paid
no one will save
the army who lived

did he spread our tears
did he save our unity
did he shape our fear
or merely hurt for country?

"Black Week in July"

nine millimeters Satanic pierces God's word
our vision turns havoc like a starry spiral
watermelon seeds shred my insides
around my ribs wrap the vines tight

eating oreos to hide the blood in my stool

every drop's a memory that'll fade
like babies in blackout NICU
don't forget to cough the h sounds
when you say van Gogh

pick up watermelon, if they still have it,
oreos by the box
don't forget the trojans
and sabra

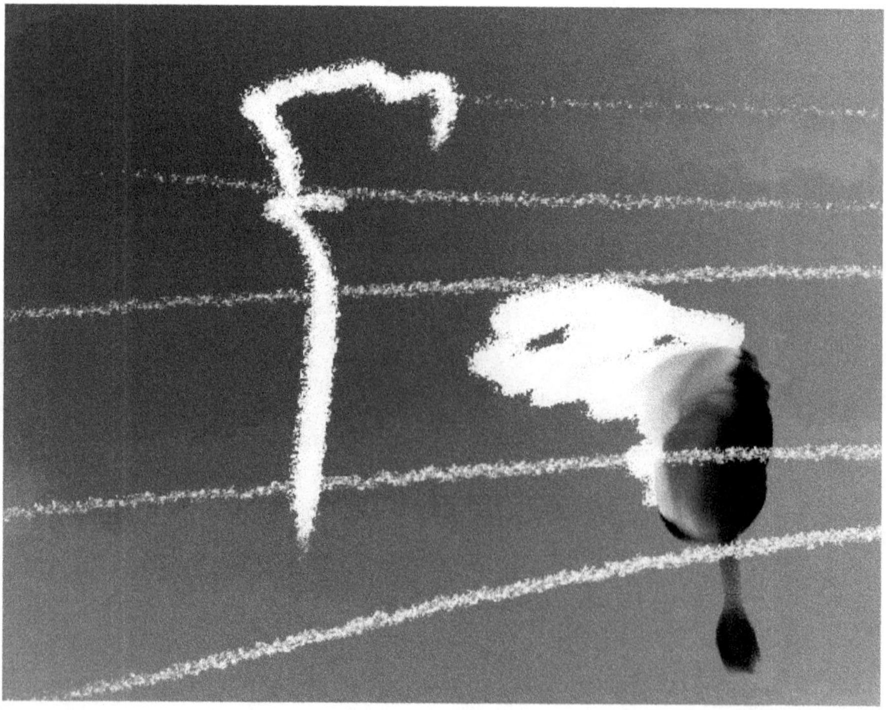

"9 11 24"

1
My young hand reached for that poinsettia.
Her beauty was fuzzy enough to tickle
but my pinching finger felt the plastic
and I never again longed for red petals.
2
If I can choose to dream away life
and I can deaden all feeling inside
then my sexuality can be despised
without becoming philophobic.
3
My inner rage was more than Corgan's rat.
Super-systemic, I let it ferment my every sweet
into a tonic sour and toxic. Given as gifts,
even as my elixir brought blood to my nose.
4
I never learned how to show my pearly lies
but compassion forged bonds anyway.
Despite my hateful highs and inward lows
children of the repressed named me friend.
5
They were good as any I'd known.
They gave me sanctum when I was lone
and when those planes became weapons
a nation chose to name them aliens.
6
The crying eagle demands I hate Arabs.
The wrinkled despots sell me war profits
in exchange for excessive civil liberties
until justice is colored the same as bone.
7
My Gen X sympathies only serve to date me.
There is no accepted doctrine of coexistence.
Even oppressed friends now preach division,
for what was human is now ethnicity.

8
And the blood runs faster than it ever had.
My own may boil but I chew my cage.
One tragedy replaced the memory of war
as we celebrate racism's makeover turning 23.
9
I thought my heart was dead to pain
but that only allowed hatred to foster,
and the atrocities of yesterday
defend the war crimes of today.
10
In 26 days we celebrate another tragedy,
reconfigured like a woman stuffed in a fridge,
inspiring patriotic murder and vindictive jokes,
elaborating how torture is preferable to nukes.
11
I thought my heart had cried no more
but love opened that clichéd entrance.
Now I get to feel shame for my race,
for my nation,
for my legacy,
for my air I don't deserve to breathe.
12
My own isolation,
my meager betrayal,
my paranoid seething is teaming with spite,
but I don't deserve to feel any injustice,
not when our capital censures what's right.
13
My fight has died before it ever began
because we gave up our voice to prop up Reagan
and Nixon and every single corporate shill that sold
liberty for votes while the Christian pogram retooled
Sondheim and every other song line into status quo
reinforcing garbage until it fits perfect in plastic wrap
that goes well with the snacks we fill with corn starch

because our forefather's political children traded artful
nudes for stipends that moved the corporate line beyond
the protections of people so that we're not close to equal
and the idea of unions preaching evil is undisputed reality
cause profits are rights of the elite but the poor shouldn't eat
and I'm made to feel guilty for throwing a coke can in the trash
when the fat cats can belch gas and repurpose fresh water
miles away into droughted lands to sell feel-good-now lite by
the six pack and even a credible threat of all life doesn't exist
as mansions erode into shores cause frogs that don't want to
be boiled shouldn't be thrown into pots and I'm not allowed
to speak to say things how I feel they should be said cause
my inflections must be poised my punctuation understood my
poetics simple to reach the masses but not the drab who speak
double negatives and how'd it come to this where people raised
in projects can't speak their subjective truth without being
called uncouth cause their skin isn't white but it lacks enough
pigment to keep them segmented off from the art of the street
where they live while poverty is promoted as a feature that
defines Black life three terms after the forty-fourth disaster
vacated his office to a criminal who should not represent this
land let alone set policy for the people who will willingly vote
for an admitted rapist who already tried to remove the last lie
that this democracy thrives.

14

All of that,
yes, all of that,
is an iceberg's tip
to the injustices we live.

15

With patriotic bluster,
they vowed to remember.
I have not forgotten the speed
with which hatred destroys kindness.

16

They named it an

emergency to justify
a call to action and when
that failed they lied and spent.
17
And the totality
of my adult years
saw not one person punished
for launching a campaign of blood.
18
Yet they demanded
my memory, so I still think
about how those heroic first responders
had to fight for care with the help of a comedian.
19
Every year I am reminded
that God has no love for this country
that hate crimes make for great punch lines
that pretty lies lack substance while devaluing truths

"Gobble"

my attempt at kindness a precursor to blind rest
but I wake from this drawl cushioned by pins
threaded by tubes
a weakness within bonding to glue
in the veins and again it's the same

cuz of hearts bleeding rocked
by a flag black with hate
and a daughter of immigrants
grants grifters chamber powers
to plant the seed of tomorrow's deceit
to give state decrees
to decide who women should carry
and what nutrition
they steal cuz the billionaires
own every red cell

I fill up a bottle
with the hope to reach an outta
this world soul drifting by fists pummeled purple
one smile with orange juice
gonna send foxes to chicken coops
and we ain't got wire fence 'fore the wicked get their rest

what was once will come again
and this barrage of wrecked hens
needs a donation or that end
coming fast
too soon
I got enough to lose
but my flaws subsume
every spark of good intent

so I'm back again
with cracked eyes and pen
and this long shout within

ain't getting softer friend

I need a surgeon's hand
to find a moment within
but this wrecked arm is bent
carved up like native trust

my bonesaw's gone to rust
cause no fuckers gonna put me up
by a table of broken treaties
defending Jackson's legacy
while they're chewing on gray meat

pale by purpose
silent with shame
a discount nurse's verses
confirm how I'm spending that day
"Child abuse," sums up decades of decay
but our nods don't meant squat
to the trail our president sprayed

pick a people
choose a culture
flip pages through the past
find a tragedy
read a summary
of this nation cashing in death

and we've had a long juicy year
of vengeance to fatten up this feast
be thankful for cranberry
while our bombs light up the East
let every rocket give praise
to a nation drawn by broken treaties
clasp hands and think of family
while racists paint our streets

no flu or
achoo

more reasons for Asian hate
sports ball
small talk
and another year of Nakba
soon every grandpa won't predate the cleansing
lick the plate clean before the last touchdown
wait for a word from the fear mongers you trust

then do it all again in three weeks
when a baby with a message of peace
gave humanity the zeal to starve infants
and punish every child for being less
than a standard never set
but always enforced
so don't forget that last course

packed in plastic built by slaves
from overseas cause those cowards
in Washington once voted for liberty
good thing the union is moving on
from that dictate of public decree
now guns will cast the votes
the side with the most bodies wins

so I begin to speak dark like a prophet
but embody no spirit nor eye of tomorrow
my sulking rants an epitaph of how I sorrow
I tap crooked alone missing the tang of gossip
I watch a flickering phone only collectors ring
in a simmer I sow a necktie from obsession
as words of lost bonds shorten my measure

but I drink water to flush toxins
I mix bone into warm tonic
eating life to keep sobbing
these sacced costs must justify
every breath that I suck
out this ball determined to end

our infectious spread
but still I defend
our right to pick lice
and fight for figs
cuz we on the rock for the long haul
and science ain't saving shit

"Procrastination"

this sky is *too beautiful* to kill myself
thankfully I live in SoCal and the ash will return

people survive eating *flour* caked with blood
it would be *presumptive* of me to do any less

now that I know bullets can only be heard in one direction
and that muskets are *louder* than bombs

it's a fact that a *trepanned* temple is more holey
than a pun that attacks Christian hypocrisy

maybe *transubstantiation* can happen in reverse
and we will bake wine cakes with the muzzle heat

maybe I'll burn my skin *before* Plath's gas
gives me my poetic end and I'll scramble out the oven

yet the sky is *beautiful* for a reason
this is how God celebrates genocide

"Insane Age"

all this pain and stale rage
in an age where insane
buys small clout for your name
all my rhymes sound the same
and opines shout hoarse refrain
cuz I got squat blocks bet on games
of tall tales without fame
and those shot clocks blinking tame
when this locked box clicks again
let Pandora rip hope out my cage

I don't wish for the best cuz doom's a better partner
every bright tune a lyrical tool make me blind to a poor after
but when the gullible grow flush from wandering star struck
I believe they've won til curtains drop
to show the wizard hawking poppies
and I gotta keep on this road of gold
while the bricks aren't sold
cause a world ending generative chatter
got the world's richest investing in the shatter

I never wanted to be ground meat but I got more than small beef
with all these well framed wet cheeks talking trash
on suffering necessary to endure to make ends meet
cuz these masks ain't styling but tools for fey wandering
if you claim you partner with me then put that torch down
form community
but you too busy partying

with sycophants to look past your sub count rising
and ponder damage caused by viral bling

while you out there milking despair from sympathetic ears
the rest of us gotta keep our heads down
and make sure our thoughts aren't heard
you think that ain't deep
look at celeb trials
to see how this public really thinks

ain't a day go by where I don't imagine blood in the kitchen
the knife's tip is tempting while I'm washing dishes
and the sponge brings back pure fun hearing unearthed traumas living
from a mom whos got soft until the tissue starts itching
she don't drop bombs but my shadow stains those walls
I don't fall
I don't breathe
just bite my cheek and grind teeth
eyes hard on suds and clean
every stain a reason to not be

my existence is writ red a bank statement full of debt
a legacy of hard regret and poverty my mouth begets
with every chip and every steak and every chance I didn't take
forming a life of foul ends where all who knew me are better spent
so I let their ghost fade fast as those close are scorned to last
cuz my last bond on this ball is my only chain
to this age where insane goes untreated anyway

"Critical Edge"

"I don't care" is such a blatant lie
used to hide the drama of success
but the p r i d e of good character
        arguments churning
so the other   side is commerce
that we were bred to c u d with
four stomachs and none covered

that s i l v e r lining is frequently
a sugar glaze helping yesterday's
meat go down with pop and shot

but as one crop w a v i n g to another
I wonder how much metal we swallow
it's not about putting specks   in stew
            diagnosis requires
going elbow d e e p   in   droppings
and so I armor up, sharpen, and hunt
stopping to review c o l d gashes

playing   devil's bitch   and gnat alike
in the hopes that a thorough butchering
keeps   e n o u g h
                                        truth to see where
      my optic center needs to be severed

or the median and extremes are all "fine"

"At Home Test"

placing your tongue between your teeth
is a verified way of tasting the weight
on your shoulders and fighting tmj
knowledge of such chronic stress conditions you may
wish to enumerate a list of all potential symptoms

as the culminated clog of failures
have been known to predate the loss of all civil rights
however it should be known that the fashion
is to flash your weakness
forgoing the securities you bought with liberties
in a show of mistaken masculinity that happily applies
to women and all future oppressed classes

thus as long as you taste between oil and copper
your metallicity is at an acceptable level to splurt
into a plastic bottle to then be contaminated
dehydrated and reinjected in a circulature
better suited for pain than altruism

all others should consult a magician
as you may be in a realm that I wish to inhabit
or so close to dead that necromancy is required

"I Know Why the Poor Kid Subscribes"

All caged birds don't sing.
Poor feathered beings
need more than water and seed,
but pellets, fruit, and affection.
Their song comes not from hard need
but empathy, care, and dedication.
Every melody is their gift.

So why is this concept so bereft
in the conversations we, homo sapiens,
place upon the imprisoned avians?
Little heads, mean simple minds.
Yet even when science proves this a lie
we despise the allegation that our cage
is anything but a life sublime.

Every zoo is full of food and their healthcare
can't be beat. Literally, no alternatives exist.
Yet we persist and this myth to save our wounded
conscience is not altogether honest.
We enjoy the power of life and death.
We enjoy the struggle of wills, the endless test
of our autonomy over what we have claimed.

But I'm being lame. We've all thought the same.
Zoos and pet stores aren't made of horrors.
They're held together by childhood splendor.
Of course, lately their spending sprees
don't go much further than a smiling tablet.

And that's the magic of living in this meta-lie
we've named "late stage" so that revolutionist
dreams can seem to have answers. Haven't I
been forthright enough to give you the contents
of my squishy lobe frontal? Well this tissue

is twisted by the insipid destiny of the kids's

who stream to be a subject on camera.
I think that's the panorama: the twinkling
shine that illuminates across our time.

Animals farm,
they even sacrifice,
but among
their myriad forms,
we alone bring sentience

to atrophied progress.
Cause repressed singing
makes perfect sense,
to a species born
in service.

"In Their Masquerade"

In their masquerade
we were hiding by
washing our brains.
Every twilight,
dawn's last pain
became a distant
lamenting refrain.
All the children
laughing so gay
chipping stone walls
adorned in gold hate.
Did we summer
in our modest cave
only to wake
in a barren winter?

Did we splinter from the cause
drinking wine and smoking thots
replacing Mommy dearest
with another passion thief?

In their splendor, at their balls,
rubbing elbows, counting cards,
never noticing our pots
paid tithe to the House.

All the chips behind the scene
filled up coffers, fat with greed,
while we cherished sweet
complimentary praise.

Drunk on bubbles, stoned on hash,
tagging stragglers with our laughs,
we tried roasting piggies
in the farmer's courtyards.

We found no treasure at the X,
no faces booked behind the mask,
but at least they saved us
boxseats
for the show!

In their masquerade
we all dance as we
shiver afraid.
Wear your skin proud
to your grave
another color
bleached the same
as death's pallor.
Add a tear to the rain
maybe streets will
clog at the drain
and last season's
sanitized brain
will rake free
a whirlpool of shame.
In our dawning fate
they wait for you.

Here's your ticket for two.

"Unwinnable"

in the mental health game we fold every hand
bemoaning our shared fate from the sidelines
of our own lives but what if we rob the house

there is more than art sharing a long sob
those beaten crippled crawled tall
diligent minds identified winning cards

we need not smother calm reprieves
we are a congress of likeminded biology
we all long for friends to recognize pain

our laments combat the prevalent apathy
they are messages floating on strained devotion
and preemptive supplication to defuse fury

face that punishing hate until it gives way
to a truth that lends voice to frustrated hearts
the blueprints of bliss need not be drafted fresh

we have a world's chorus to join when we sing
ten thousand years of teachers who persevered
a humble sum who longed to not be forgotten

Unwinnable DX???

An earlier raw version on "Unwinnable" is available in the book's dissection section. You can read "proto Unwinnable" on page 276.

"No Sanctum"

So blind with pride, can't even match the wing shape
to the hallowed highs scribbled on soft birthright.
Perceived divine was a sanctum for cloud rats.
Their squeaked delight never seen past Father's hate.

Lifting sharp time only to examine what years obscured.
Myopic fixation to the witworn plan that treasure provides,
that jigsaw past found from resealed shards lost in tragic
woes for a future only obtained through maladies's cure.

Every break from expectation ignites rage to tantrum.
Pushing possibilities off by frustration for scorn's sake.
Seeing halo's lack as reason to start Armageddon's fight,
ignoring how conviction's rubble leaves no sanctum.

"Countup"

one you see
torn by sick heaven
hate shine sent
depression helps
dirty fortunes between
sickly sanctity racking
nightly trends clean

fun you've seen
born sick with longing
diamond dreams
made cheap by scrut'y
favored cleaned
in garbs of plenty
washing mean
with scripts *all knowing*

eye

seeing all
you should buy

hate light sent
depression helps
to mud the pain
and gray the self
outsiders lend
relief from jail
their foreign mien
a banner for *all knowing*

mouth

screaming how
they lie by truth

dirty fortunes between
the light and the hate

the right and the grave
and our life
can't be bought
but it's on sale
tonight

given a lease
won't you be pleased
when your intro rate
decreases to zero
no more heroes
blocking their delight

come and buy a grave
you want
security for the lame
and the blind
who'll be there to
prick them when you climb?

all seeing eye
separate the night
from this dusk
aren't you tired
of tasting rust?

all screaming mouth
tell us all how
do we speak ascent?
there is a wrong way
to agree with them

sanctity racking
nightly trends clean
divine ads protecting
what the children stream
foxes haunting
the mind coops clean

yesterday omelettes
a feather fiend
filled up your pantry
but you have to eat
a million ghosts
offering you a sheet

all knowing light
why must your shine
blind us in bed
don't the weary
also need some rest?

all seeing eye
separate the white

all screaming mouth
tell us how to bow

all knowing light
teach us what's right

all purchasing stocks
tell us when we're bought

"Doom Colored"

dread days don't come
they honor you to stay
to take up residence
in the hopes of yesterday

nibbling on what wasn't said
making cushions of frayed fun
entertained by thumbed solace
any day their home will be ours

on the casket
by Damascus
drove into mom's heart

feel the brackets
in the attic
shuttering from foul arts

in the pipes
on the lawn
over cobble
across dawn
where the first drops
of the alms lost
in a sea screaming far

did you blink light
or was that shadow

always
on your arm

dread not that pinching ring
nor the hissing burn of rain
noon sulfur calls your name
ain't petrichor dull to tame

when the whips of winds can't keep the foul get out

won't the bawling infants ever
get
out

all the scars of promises
need more cocoa butter salves and an honest
hitch in your jaw
do they expect you to pitch from the lawn?

after Wednesday debts are accrued
have you tires left to zoom
or will you spend time to delay
that inevitable unenviable regrettable fate
where inedible nights bring ache in bed
from children eating guilt instead

while those day long guests
repurpose clutter into corner offices
and all those tiny sins
give donation for pulpits
so the doom colored robes fit
in the mind stress made vacant

as those one time visitors ascend
to the highest office of your coffin
you spend your final days at home
writing an ideal proposal
for the downsizing of your life
to mere memories of those
who haven't lost the love inside
but cry not

they aren't far behind

"scent of my soul"

miasma of death she called to me
sin made painless by prophecy
every step by every boy
becomes a task becomes a chore
for the one who spun the world
to spin to dread

oh humble weakness she set me free
in the thrashing of my pit I wept gently
but the sting of every tear
from every eye of every boy
is a drop in the waterfall named
Victoria

searing in the heat of my regret
I crawled up the pit of loneliness
and every hand that touched my arm
pulled me up to dust me off
wasn't sent by a book that
no one read

the women of the stars they dazzle me
cruel, gentle, and smart, they start a beat
in every heart of every boy
that endures pain while ignoring joy
but they were made second declares
a copied page

miasma of death she clings to me
I wanted nothing less but harmony
demands that I pay for my crimes
that never burst out from my mind
in actions but that fat man
in the clouds
won't allow
my step

"Gordita Supreme"

90s kids will remember,
the prediction of disaster.
The flood of digital fun
would turn us to babies
whining for nutrients,
unable to log off.

They were mocked.

As the digital age was birthed
on a stage of trickle down ego,
honest grifts that popped
a "dot com bubble" before
ambit' homeowners took
"loans they couldn't afford."
From the bitch to the fad,
it was never the street bad
but the wall stayed esteemed
as bits raised home prices
to rates of real estate cream.

Our prize for this eco bomb fest?
Shamed for living off X and babies
as their gen complained of welfare state.
Patriots acting with laughs
as votes regained the right
to be held back by a test,
since racism is dead.
It was killed by cultural segregation,
co-opting a cry for sensitivity
into a mantra of deniability.

Appropriately, the hate lived on.
Growing from buzzy exclusion
to homeland superiority
in the time it takes to read

presidential crime records:
about twenty years
and a bottle of *Stolichnaya.*
Now they'll come to find ya,
online for ancient memes
or outside for alien genes.

But the 90s are back!
Don't have a cow,
put that stick
in your bunga!

Bell and Taco's Excellent Ad Venture
revives the Gordita Supreme,
eyeliner, goth 'tude, and black shirts
from a band enthusiast's wet dream.
Who minds if the scene is dom'd
by the same Princess? Kids like Nirvana,
we can resurrect slut shaming!
Re-up the corp grifting.
Pepsi's got Harvey Danger
raging against the machine with 'zines!
The revolution starts with a cravings box!

While the kids who walk our walk
are trained by lower class drains
soaking up donation. A full tenth
of their grind is reading simp lines
alongside their bits and sub times
cuz their hot takes are fast breaks
from the cultivates shakes
of academic excellence screaming
from their own grave,
but kids get that strong dope hit
for every mention of their name.
As legislation comes for loot
but cravings don't stop in that box.

"Budding Fame"

Adult sins repackaged for kids
gets a pass by adding laughs
on a studio track. Teen

thighs bared, a scandal exposed
and we all act shocked. Closeups
on lips, sassy comebacks and swaying
hips, and we think the young safe

when the camera stops.
Starlets smile at their sexy
debut and fans wonder
where their morals flew.

"Run With Me"

Take a run with me.
Feel the ground push.
Exhale. Kiss the breeze.
Shake off the soothe.
It's a race we can't lose.
Doubt never falters,
got the shrill speed of shadow
that brings what's in without.

Don't concentrate on gains.
Lose the rhythm of your hurt.
No long heat needed to escape.
You ever   w o n d e r

why dreams aren't born when we're older?
Does reality play more than a soft interference?
We praise a steadfast adherence to a vision,
but if dedication only festers into sorrow
does will form the bars of our prison?

How do we mend hollow
ambition without a salve
of success? Maybe it's time
to call this long race to rest.

But these feet still rise.
My mouth still breathes.
We got streets to ride
and grass to murder
concrete tragedies
that need to go further.
For these thousand families
surrounding our borders

are a glint in the alley to show where carnage happens,
a splinter of a tree cracked wide by lightning,
a flicker of a flame deprived precious oxygen,
and all their caution falls when doors are strong,
until they fence with words we all alone running.

Take a run with me.

"fences"

Weather worn brick or rusty chainlink, all the lawns
were weeds and the green faded. Another dog barks
and soon screams the baby. The only white fences
here are in a heart grown heavy. For they lost their spark
when the dream went dark and I ain't never kicked a pug

when it ran for my leg.
But you know I weren't fittin
to be alone on that pavement.

Cuz the beer and the gas was all
they can swallow, when the sugar
killed their liver and they can't afford
a bottle of juice from the sow
sold by the biggest pig of all.

Allowed by the scam of the house
deader than bone. Cuz Banting sold
a cure for a single working dollar,
and that dollar's worked harder
than a poor man's father.

While the next generation can't afford
a home and TV sets polish regret
with the nightly drama.

But I ain't been the one that had to walk
through that door. My complex
a government annex of flea filled floors.
And every cent they spent made a condo
built to creak so that every lousy flower
was cut down to concrete.

Still we just like them wasting
hours; getting flabby by our habits
cause the static went with HD
but the garbage in our head

was inherited for free.

So there weren't nothing special about living
behind a gate cept there were fewer of us
here to spread around the hate. Every scam
was still a lure we were sure to bring salvation.
With no church we knew hurt
was our final destination.

And I ain't never asked nobody to assist. The rackets from their boss
got them blind to a grift. Cuz every fuck with plastic got a smile on their dollars. It's in our pocket now but they the ones that make it holla.

make it holla
make it holla
make it holla

We scream
from the dream
they painted on our brains
and the scene
ain't complete
until we're dancing on TV.

on daddy reveals when the cheater cries
we dancing
on the news when the crime rise
we dancing
at takeover when tires fry
we dancing
at mass when the children die
we shaking

cuz we ain't gonna take it all
and they be sellin our stylin
when our convictions fall

"summer death"

summer
feel the pulse rise
as sweat irritates

heat
churning filth to fertile
transient state

ash
falling from a golden
dropless sky

death
made immortal through
tragedy's ebony lines

summer
a feeling all around
that glory's wicked

heat
taking names, signing sheets
as the blazes form

ash
from the homes of those
opulently fitted

death
falling to the lungs
where the crow caws

summer

a cheap mirage made dirty
by sods calling people
to a sequel of constitutional
fraud. Lesser equals

heat

buying evil for goods
and no services rendered
can tender their resig-
nation of hating.

ash

The cause of violence,
a radical pipeline
buying up silence
through radios hijacked

death

by the dreams of free peons
made blood soaked by
"can't we let bygones"
for crimes no one denied.

summer

Yet the game stays
the same, when liberty
is shredded by each foray
of slander that's made tame

heat

by the thousands of pamphlets.
Distributed like bombs
though the smoke may not clear
we got patriotism in our song.

ash

That won't last past a cleaning
of crimes washed down to lies.
So that cornflakes still crunch
while they're signing off with goodbye.

Death

comes for us all when the morning reporting
pairs with mountain grown
beans, made creamy and sweet
by the smiling faces predicting
violence on the street.

summer
heat
ash
death

summer
heat
ash
death

Summer brings the *heat* to keep *ashes* from *death*
that won't come from a mushroom or a whimper
but a people that simper and suck who they serve
and say "thank you" to the Lords who leave

one scrap for their family.
How's about gravity
right itself some sanity
and bring the wicked to their fall?

Will this fucking season ever change?

"Fang of Another"

Fang of another
knocked loose from a jaw.
Brain in the gutter
spread grit for the fall.
Pain is a mother
gotta bleed for the job.
Time gonna smother
your heartstring's song.

My confidence
gone limp from heat.
Them rallying steps
soft at the knees.

An army we make,
well, I'm a soldier of fake.
The violence we start
got no room for a march.

Been yappin' and actin' like all the trouble
we can't see ain't got no effect on me.
Those people in the steeple ain't that real when we got steel
cages upgraded to half-full class and luxury flats,
and the fat cats who have all that I've ever wanted--
but I can watch them glitter in their golden chat.
All the real songs ain't heard in so long
that we got bitches thinking that protests long gone,
like some absurdity from the
crazy bad-trip hazy recollections
of the feckless art that couldn't start
a revolution if it sucked
back up they ass from every shart.

And I know you think it's funny
to laugh about our death.
Take a selfie on your way down,

scream your last breath.
All the cows limp like lambs
towards the shadows of a tree.
Rot has frayed the green
leaving cruciform sentry.

If dynamite's in the mix then
how come you sounding off a hiss?
Cuz that green cactus
the only shit that's blowin' up
but you got Steves turning off
the blast of the ghast cause you want

what's built to last.
We're so averse to setbacks
that a replay off our own stage
is tolerable cause our foibles

are made to give shame;
for an audience we can't contain.
Cuz ain't none of us choose
our privacy to loose in a batch
before oranges memeing angry
they signed a patriot act. All they
talking heads said it was good for gand
but what's grander than a gander
that honked loud and took a stand;
but we can't.

These fucking kids
can't even conceptualize a world
that won't cater to their demands
and they take smiles fake and click
buttons that shake endorphins
like crack fiends before they

even had a wet dream.
How you think they gonna rule this crate,

when the impact of our failure
made a cradle for hate,
or are you gonna tell me
that moderate Rogans got the slate
wiped clean? You'll fight me
for speaking up against a pipe dream
that all the pipes sucked lean
ain't gonna spin you round and pound
your last words of consent to keening sound.

Fang of another
knocked loose from a jaw.
Brain in the gutter
spread grit for the fall.
Pain is a mother
gotta bleed for the job.
Time gonna smother
your heartstring's song.

You follow me?
Don't bother me.
I got cake to eat my fate
in a diabetic ending.
See, I ain't the martyr you need
or a speaker for cold bodies.

The second you like my page
twenty others gonna fill your brain,
this cascade of information rocks
your station, making every patient
thought gestating a patient read
no survival chance cause screens
weren't built to last and the photons
blinking on y'all optic balls
gonna seal what it don't steel
like a woolly mammoths off the grill;
I'm talking tar that leaves no scar

but there's plenty left to heal.

I ain't a doctor just a premature cor'ner.
This ain't the prophecy you need,
but I'm your bum begging for order.
I'm hear to warn you,
but mine ain't nothing special
so I'll cash in your pity.
Need me to sweeten the deal?
Build no statues in your half-used
sanctum of serenity where your sanity lasts.

Fang of another
knocked loose from a jaw.
Brain in the gutter
spread grit for the fall.
Pain is a mother
gotta bleed for the job.
Time gonna smother
your heartstring's song.

"Papercuts"

papercut
over bone tracing
the line one finds
between
arm hairs and bare
skin too thin
but thick enough
to keep viscera
under the faded
indigo

the travels I troubled the news scans I bubbled
with bluebirds and emotes spoke nothing to power
save the carbon we squandered
and borrowed
interest with no regrets so that insects below
their last instar went far from home
but never to loam only soil baked dry
from a boil

of a blue world
gone to flames
never they sold souls
with any shame
cuz t'ain't gray matter
to speak through pain
when eyes open burn to stay
in that state cause the state
protects hate through
constitutional claims

in the jungle of life and death past the city where angels rest they wings get sold for seven-seventy by the offramp of congealed dreams emerge slowly when given a little bit of stake but when money parts the gel it's the cell that they share where every bitter fucker starts some hell

and the paper
drags up over knobs
where the elbows
can't extend to defend
cuz a life on keys
have no need to pick free
the parasites from their face
or the pleasure center
which has no purpose
anyway

all the things you love can be bought at the store
if it wasn't do you want it anymore
are you sure
cuz we got buttons to like and subscribers to buy
friends to follow and victories to survive
the haters ain't got justice to stand on
they need more hours to pamper
the icons we serve
ain't they learn
that harmony is all music not spiritual practice
life's absurd

and that lacerating edge
y'know it's comin' for the head
but not the wires that bleed
see they don't use no one's voice
but there's a stockline to replete
cuz that paper's goin' towards
that info center

just remember
to agree to all terms
and that fine print is glint
you got power to conserve
all trees they chop

all process back to
paper

papercut from the bone
to the hinges
up they necks
until no one's next

"Arctangent's Tail"

The old god is gold but we pray to plastic
too. Problem is the text within is gambling
on national roulette. Every time that ball
stops the bottom class foots the debt.

Funnier than an oncologist with
cancer is an economist talking math.
Macro means *no bueno* for rebates
on land rates and CEOs help good
greed flow so interest topples principals.

Here's an encore:
Film scripts and WSJ got something in common
one brain indie games beat their truth to bottom.
Beaten by an auto clicker writing thicker without
words on the screen. See they know commerce
can't grow annually without demolishing the
system, but the fiftieth spun solar revolution
marks when Welsh sacced mercy for wealth.

So the ticker tape rat race goes to space
while estates take over three quarters
per dollar for American place worked
harder than any part timer could ever haste.
An economy laid waste is always blamed on
foreigners to exploit; domestic or over shore;

and they mad that a living wage means a line
at rest. Instead of recognizing that exponential
growth exists only when you bring the viewing
scale down low. For all things have an upper
limit. True gains follow the tail of an arctangent.
Still execs don't rec this the ceiling they're pushing.

So they drop billions on ideas squeezed
drier than their eyes and blame diversity
when their staff and crew ain't got time

to follow through.

Market cannot live off hype alone.

Eventually their promises must materialize
a throne, but there's only so much gold to scatter.
Their coffers are sealed too tight to trickle
When the people need a deluge to pay for extra pickles.

Still not convinced about the destruction
they risk? Why you think they're giving layoffs
to workers that brought record gains?
Or burying finished products earning write offs
for their names? While pundits pissed on primetime
about welfare feeding fams. They got a bribed
political system hiding total failure.

Stocks and bonds are frauds from cons.
There's no product bought,
no service prolonged.
It's all stories where the plot
is tricking the rich to buy in.
Now egg on the face is the fashion,
making movies to dramatize disaster.
For this age of sunk cost fallacy
can't stop producing tragedies.

"Drowsy Days"

My fantasy role
is hitting big style.
The sum of our gold
ain't breaching the wilds
of gray waylaid by
daily single file
marching to graves.
We all seen them while
the fuse missed its mile.
A stare barely there
'til a screen can share

the 'moji we hardly can't be 'til the feed tells us how we breathe.
Let that sink to the drink of an epiphany bubbling
from a fermentation born of degradation, unnamed
and untried, but the masses don't deny
the sulfur inside 'til we all swear there's a yellow outline.

I'm cutting no rug
but crawlin' up glass.
Each rip makes a slit
for infection lasts
past ointments solvent
small pain. Summer drags
over blue skies flowing
and night's drowsy drug.

"13 Presidents Why"

Turn the faucet off these six hour baths.
Lock your roofs up and weather this fall.
We got a lot of winter to bite,
don't let this be terminal.
Our stripes have gone black
so our hearts need its blood.
We got better use for rope
and that doom can stop scrolling.
It's gonna end free thought,
with or without you joining.
We got a fire to blaze
so find the fuel deep in you.

I know there's a hate for injustice
and you trust us to be there
when good fails, but we gotta be
demons who are cool, when hate
rips down our neighbors,
ice the opposition
not with reason
but by seizing the same bonds
and safeties that these fearmongers
have been shaping since flowers
lost power by being symbols of tomorrow.

No. Nobody gonna cut a lobotomy out of these chumps.
We gotta be the ones to stop the mechanisms of state
from letting white sheets dictate what they legislate.
So take all these lumps, protect what's in vogue to beat.

Plan not a pardon for the crooks that blood these streets,
but be the people who march on our liberties.
Join the blue. Jump in the slop. Eat donuts with Wiggum.
I don't give a fuck if all of them are bastards.
We need a clear conscience when they name a new target,
cuffs that bind fists so they won't continue an onslaught.
Them courts that you despise, who misshape our lives?
We gotta have skin in that game so that a jury can thrive.
Without a judge who'll see past the skin and see needs
that drive crime without giving in to blind disdain.

We need our people to be united in resistance,
to fight smart while they contort morality.
Our call for peace gave them lawns to breach.
Their sovereignty the start of some lawless insanity?
Well develop a complex called the left in fatigues.
Their military industry needs bodies to oil metal.
Send our children to their boots; fight in their league.
Let pride die as we remind them how feuds get settled.
Add some shade to our army's complexion
because an army of one shouldn't mean one people.
We may be divided but we need to rep our nation.
It can't just be at pulpits, we gotta enlist. Find the will!
The diversity they need can't be merely skin deep.
If we only preach peace, they'll commit perfidy.
The second amend is meant to stop the bleed.
When their mobs come we can defend our city.

This is still America and we are still a nation,
but the left can't just be blue. We must be red
with rage and include the white. That color

must be more than evil it's gotta contain allies.
Give up your bias. Tolerate microaggressions.
Laugh at sick jokes but be there as protection.
Our culture war is lost. Whether Vladimir or John
we have to stop singing their songs.
Lennon is dead and he was killed for the fame.

So imagine a world where the left is more than a voice.
We can't just be sign holders that march where they permit.
We must be their brothers so they cry when we end.
We have to be their coworkers, their cops, their friends.
I know they blood your boil and make funerals of the innocent
but the white sheets aren't all of them, we must alter our cause.
They've defined the battlegrounds, shown the victory.
Unless we're in their churches they will not hear you.
It's a hopeless world inherited, I know none of this is easy.
Get on your knees in prayer and know God is silent.
This is no call to be violent, but a light on our absence.
We can't fix government when we're balanced by elephants.
Laws are still around without two-thirds to shut em down.
So mend this hurt within their bubble, show you matter too.

"Dark Their Light"

I've known hard shock from loss
before breathing relief from death
misty ghosts give quiet company
whilst people haunt my evenings
where lives are saved I tremble
mercy costs far more than aches

for years now I sleep in beds
but that sense of home eludes
my unlatched heart serves better
home made me demon food
I'm sure they eat well nightly
there's always pity for the take

darkness warms deep in the cradle
light hurts eyes at rest
mouths who speak of good deeds
turn heads far from grace
next year's harvest today's dreams

no linear thought process
no compromise in between
all my shouts for justice
make me a villain on their page
they sew my lips shut slowly
like a fish drying in a cage

so I will bleed from threadlines
I will taste the metal of doubt
I will love past envy
and ache from being found

I will fail their perfect test
I will wallow in depravity
I will sing to lonely echoes
and twist the clock rabbit sees

I will walk on hottest days
and drink with hottest gays
I will be slime in their white garden
and grow in their acidic ablution

and I will know no rest
the insomniacs will unite
as long as they shame urges
we will dark their light

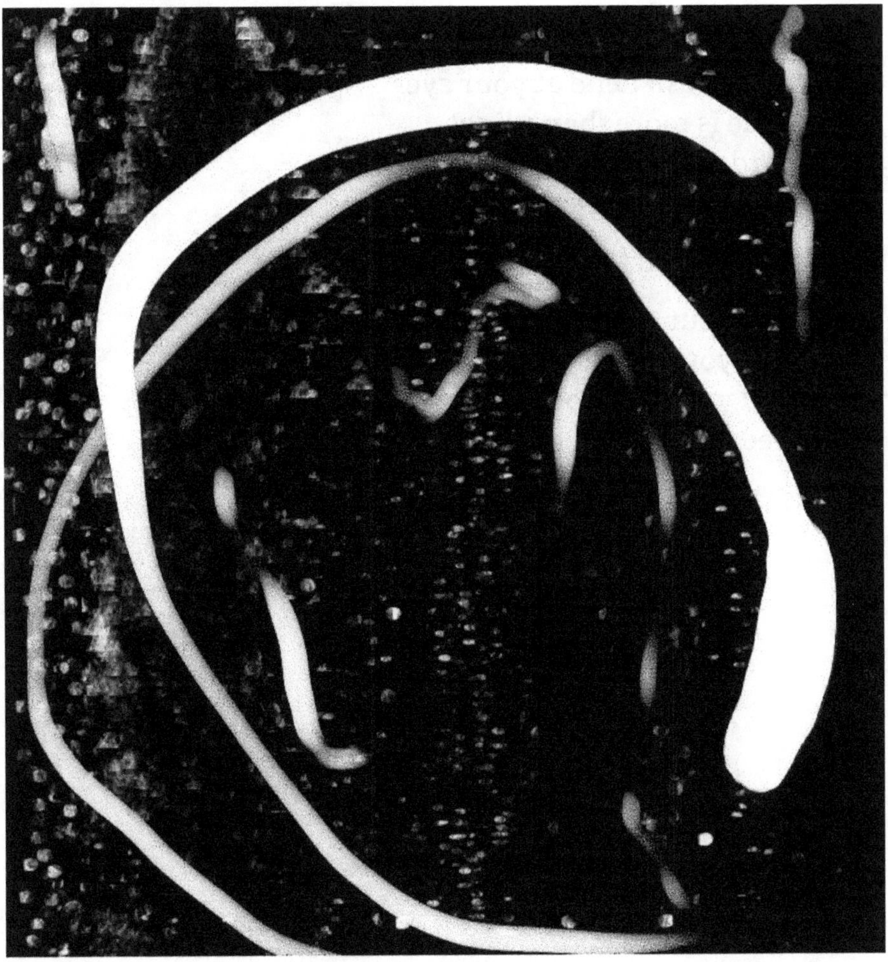

"You're Not a Log"

I see you walking wide
hear the coarse words
feel the slap and shove
smell a stink unfeminine

I get why you fear a dress

you can wear the worst
go full goblin on a raid
make yourself living trash
do nothing to impress

but you already shine

your light doesn't end at your eyes
your smile is more than a line
your words touch my heart
your thoughts inspire dark

women need you too

they need your confidence
they need your resolve
they need you to be you
they need you like I need you

because women are just like you

"Taboo Poets"

I don't write about writing as a rule
but my patience for smug has limits
I stumbled upon a saccharine smiling tool
who praised every poem in the comments
with an interchangeable vocabulary

the vid's content was advice for poets
to write their honest reactionary
insight without any rhyme or flourish

in the same vid that emboldened viewers
by encouraging them to write about brushing teeth
they gave but one taboo as a bit of overspread news
never be that girl who admits to pining lonely
do not dare speak of your pained love unrequited
this and this alone is the mark of an abhorrent
on the vid of a polished presenter perennially overexcited

I wondered with envy if they'd never known sorrow's torrent

for I have spoken to hearts drowned
by the events of adolescence
I have seen an apathy so profound
they saw no value in empathy
and through my taboo trample
of thoughts others dampened
I heard hissed by bitter laughter
how one rejection made them shatter

yet we the adults are quick to shame
to act as if our age erases pain
when all our songs repeat themes
even as we reject juvenile trends

for there is nothing crueler
than a well placed mirror
so all those whining girls
need to die a little quieter

"Homes Without Life"

we build human habitats but leave no room for life
that's why I chop down trees and kill ant lines
a thousand thinkers speculate buildings with grass
a million artists let their vision die at the press
my own home might be a flawed creation dated over fifty
but a sprawling new community is built with less creativity

in their rush to shape acres homogeneous gables rise
but they omitted walkable centers where small business thrives
there are no theaters or points of interest
they exist to be speculative real estate traps
without a single reason to live in those plots

in the glare of a shadeless patio
I stood by branches felled
the size of their totality
was greater than my self
back to the chopping I reduced logs
to a size that would fit in our cans
for even in their disposal
I must fit life to engineer plans

yet as I destroyed spider homes
and broke down a place of shade
an eastern tiger swallowtail
investigated the breezy space
in the same location I held a fresh
monarch testing hours old wings

like the ants I am more than death
the tree's soil will house milkweed
tomorrow's summer will host flowerbeds
so that caterpillars can be birthed
as the inferno sputters I'll nourish soil
and help life on this punishing earth

DELUSIONAL

"At the Butcher Block"

I was born with a knife
and ever since then I've
been trying to get it right.

The stab, the cut, the slash, the gutting out
the entrails and leaving out all that entails the innards of a
person's mind--their life, their insight, the celestial divide.

These are things I'm meant to prune and parse,
the piece that gets lost in the endless ever yawning ramble
of greeting, weather, traffic, "better get on with my life,"

because the long story short is always longer than short,
but nothing that's said is ever truly worth saying, because
the truth's not pudding, it comes in the flaying.

We are not the combined heap of our afternoon masks
and "it's not that bad," but the hurt and the pain and
all the viscera we contain. So if there's darkness to heat

our lonely night it comes in the smothering
and the womb we're denied, because
nothing's ever closer than that darkness we deny
and like light and like it all, we were born in a big
illuminating ball, a thing that's precious

and never unknowing, a pre-Planck pinion
of a phoenix reunion to this endless mortal coil
that begins not with a whimper but a boiling over
of protoplasmic goo,
to be these things that we think unnew.

For we are the future
and we buy time in bulk,
taking what's ours
and tossing the package.

Our time is like an egg that's already hatched.

The shell that was there is the darkness that's passed.
The light of our hope is a future we're blind to,
like a yolk that's bespoke to a chalazae of our sinew.
For the albumen is the acumen of a billion souls behind you

and I am but one proton
in the plasma of creation. Like all
things before me I am the beginning
and culmination.

We derive our purpose
from an instance of insight,
like a bird flying in the rain
following mountains
lit by storm light.

So when I cut, I cut deep, and I leave no lies to sleep.
I am the dividing line and the company few keep.
I apologize profusely because there's no room for me,
nor the stares that I tear from
everyone's attention turned to gloomy
past and "nothing lasts." I am the killer of presumption
and the pomp that stirs up "good enough."

When I'm gone I'll go cutting
and you'll find my knife bent,
cuz I've got a whole world to carve through
and a very sharp pen.

"My Favorite Love Trope"

I still have a hole
from heart to soul
and a limb that's limp
from a severance
never witnessed.

My mate can still wait until
forgiveness from above makes
saints of us all.
There will be no spiritual
conception, no squishy

reproduction. The thing that is me
is so obviously me and not he and
not she because people can be enby.

And it doesn't have to affect
me and doesn't redefine
me so that
my heart beats
for a thing beyond seraph wings.

There was no act of destiny, no celestial
horn or star twinkling, no zany
first encounter or mishap with a shower.

My first sight was no great delight, my sorrow
didn't reach it's twilight. My misery
made a new zenith and I found new reasons
to be less than any living thing was meant
to be, for I still long desperately
to be that skull

in a poet's great soliloquy
rather than see
the shades that haunt me.

My breath isn't bereft of the weight

that smothers glee. A love beyond my skin
didn't start within, it didn't need a hug

for one. I'm still not fun.
I'm not one in a billion

and neither is they,
but they is still fey
when compared
to the scares
of the complacent populous.

I'm done with talk of this
right and wrong and what
must come before two becomes one.

I wasn't the one,
they isn't my all,
I'm not their everything,
we are still two beings

who live
and think
and love
autonomously.

Our love is ours because
we built it with words,
we suffered past the worst
of us and had the courage to be heard.

"Love Peels"

love peels
it impacts sharp
piercing through to wound
and crack
the wall becomes a shell
and nothing stops the hatch
that solid protection
is now in pieces

and love peels
revealing bruised fruit
before slicing deep
deep enough to oxygenate
carving a grid
like an artisanal mango

and love peels
those juicy ideal sections away
one square of meaning at a time
showing the ripe interior
crushed by that initial shock
segmented along a fault

and still love peels
scraping away pulp
battered edge
and revealing that segmented heart
where every mistake
becomes tragedy
and art is torture

and still mercilessly love peels
splitting down that fault
exposing the worst of the heart
expelling thoughts like blood
rotting every tender
guarded
wicked vein within
until that once safe whole
is unrecognizable
until destruction is preferable
to living with this vivisecting decay

and life life life becomes new as birth
and it is so large that eyes water
fresh at nothing more than the sky
and every word is layered
deeper than graves
and in that anguished state
the splattered goo of self
must express without filter and wait
wait
wait for love's mercy
for that rare as comet in an eclipse
beauty that is love's return

and still mercifully love peels
revealing
some hardened core of diamond
unrecognizable as the self
and that core is a seed buried in hope

nourished by splattered self
defended by new walls
so both may grow
in tandem

sharing every drop of sun
until beauty and the pair
are one
and rubbish will find them
and parasites will infect
and dirt will cover life

and love peels that back too
leaving only the tree
half them and half you

"Mantis Kiss"

I love like a mantis offering head,
forgetting the live gift to our bed.
Instead it's juicy ideas she devours.
Still, I squander her gentle mercy.

I must cease my eager sacrifice,
finding reason beyond her eyes
to maintain my unworthy self.

To plan vacations and take comfort,
working towards an Earthly future.

"Sharing Sin"

I'm so glad I don't have to sin alone
I love the way you sin
your wickedness pricks
my civility parted by

your sinister smile
your evil burns me from within
my panting never abates
the way you make me wait
the pleasure you take from my pleading

the pleasure you take right out of me
sucking life from so deep
I feel dead down to my marrow
and with one bite
you inject back that life
and make me yearn
to sin at your command

"Love's Kiss"

expecting firm assurance
that super social bond
seemingly coded into our lips

i melt

soft
relenting
patience
rolls over my mouth
a kiss that savors
expecting nothing in return
a love so secure
it can remain unstated

accepting me in totality
should my wickedness
or sorrow
or desperate clawing neediness
surface
present they
take in a beauty
that I never feel

away from their eyes

"éclair pride"

They were mine for a moment
and though I tried to own it,
my grasp was too uncertain
to keep it secure.

Like walking through a curtain
from nervous to splendor,
I had seen all I'd needed to bite
that juicy dream, but like an

éclair from the deli
it was cold with cherry jelly,
the crust still frozen,
the custard too thin.

Blanching at the sweet kiss,
shaking back my reasons,
I saw the truth through regret's painful haze.

And the
sugar
high
rose me
past
the shame.

Over
winter
skies,
I saw
blue
over rain.

Where the Gods
and fools
and astronauts
and every sod

that bought
a spot
could fly.

Something yellow and special said,
"Goodbye."
And my

hubris lost its purpose and I began my dive.
The way down so fast it squeezed my cheeks aside.
My freefall so chilling, the tears froze to light.
And the

fog of their bad day
unfurled to rain
soaked paved
streets that shone
like night.

It was painful.
It didn't hurt me.
When despair
welcomed me

back to gravity.

"Survive the Sunrise"

too proud to beg
putting dreams to rest
all our wishes witnessed
between birth and decay

I might try to save
a few souls outta their mind
to be a kind stranger
casting one line
but this time
I feel like a fisher
hoping to reel
in compassion's glow
cuz I know
this bread's not feeding anyone

in the solitude of misery
I ain't got no patron
for my pain
and if I reach out
for a light
I find lanterns nearby

so I reach out
for as long as I can
keep on reaching out
until feeling leaves my hand
knowing my loss
creates a demand
too great
for my friends to abate
but my queer stirrings
find no shade

and so I sweat

and grit my teeth
and buy worry with my sleep
my hand close and closed
though need
shakes me dry past reason
I can only try

for so long

when I'm gone
I hope there's no goodbyes
my wrongs
don't deserve their cries
all these nights alone
burn
but survive the sunrise

"Aphonic"

Responding to a lull.
Mouth open. Ready to deliver.
Mind joined lines expressing my soul
but that pause weren't so little.
Others jumped on so I got bigger.

In the years, in the long
times I spent alone contemplating,
energy ramped up to manic.
Still my brain static override
by my pride 'til words invisible
came outside. Though I
meant none of them, stiff lip
had me spinning a defense,

and the moment came over.
Their faces weren't glazed but
never came to connect with my brain
and that shame popped back.
My jaw went snap.
Even if I was apologetic,
susurrus don't count for crap.

I try to forget it.
Try to rebuild from the shell
of the hell that was my social
solitary. What they got for me
ain't that hot, cuz peeps had
elephant minds but they speak

pleasantly.
When my brain is a bomb
it's not surprising
but it still sucks when bux
don't end the silence.

Yet it's all my scene?

Every dab and back pat
I'm committed to sorry.
Still I'm the one that gotta
keep the fire when I
ain't own a sparkler to chink.

I get aphonic.

Still it comes and goes
and trauma never shows.
If we met astral then maybe
they'd see a figure who can't
contend with harsh reality.

But new peeps shan't believe
I'm so shy my rizz in atrophy.
So they don't bother, see?
Cause a hyper fuck suffering
from a diarrhea mouth
don't count as anyone's clown.

Or a victim. Cause any vic not ideal
ain't worth a spit of lubricant
when they're shackled and sent
off to a brand new cell called
inclusion of mental divergence.

"High Intensity Technical Electronica Music"

gnashing teeth flat
wringing these hands
screaming inland
ain't no seas to span
cept being them
colony 'prehend?

my 'sire for luv it skiff all my soles
while I'm rubbin my toe
on this crowded dance floor
the failure to comm' is blame on the buzz
but 'thout the deej' mix I fuzzin' to flow

my gather'd up courage might paint me a lion
but all me long steps send me in the fryin'
so I'm back in that box where fishstick stay cold
even though I get burn
lest none think I'm worth stickin' on poles

the pike inside connect hip to my eyes
stuck up straight tho' not by my spine
the best I can manage is fittin' a line
to curve one way so they think I be lyin'
my smirk ain't no curse it's half nazar
from my soul the eyes being evil felt by ghast people

the shakin' the thrashin' it's all that come lastin'
when the flash in they pan is my crispy ego
I take longer to cook then most 'tention spans
so when we chat I ain't start to push third

'cuz my first gear take turns and veers out my hole
and there a big spot of ind'gest' mapped to vertigo
the lab'inth of my head got no exit low
so breakin' my wall the only way I can flow
but it's crammed full of garbage from stayin' a shy fool

so hit me and quit me don't lay me so cruel
that I gon' need witness to 'dentify your boot
when I fine with takin' your slap and choke
long as you leave me breath to fan coal
I'll burn this ship why you slammin' that door

said I'll burn this ship why you slammin' that door
so don't leave me limpin' but waterin' the floor
said breakin' my wall the only way I can flow
but it's crammed full of garbage from stayin' a fool
said the flash in yo' pan is my crispy ego
I'm back in that box where the fishsticks stay cold
said without that deej' mix I'm fuzzin' to flow
so next time this bumping I scuff all my soles

said hit me and quit me don't lay me so low

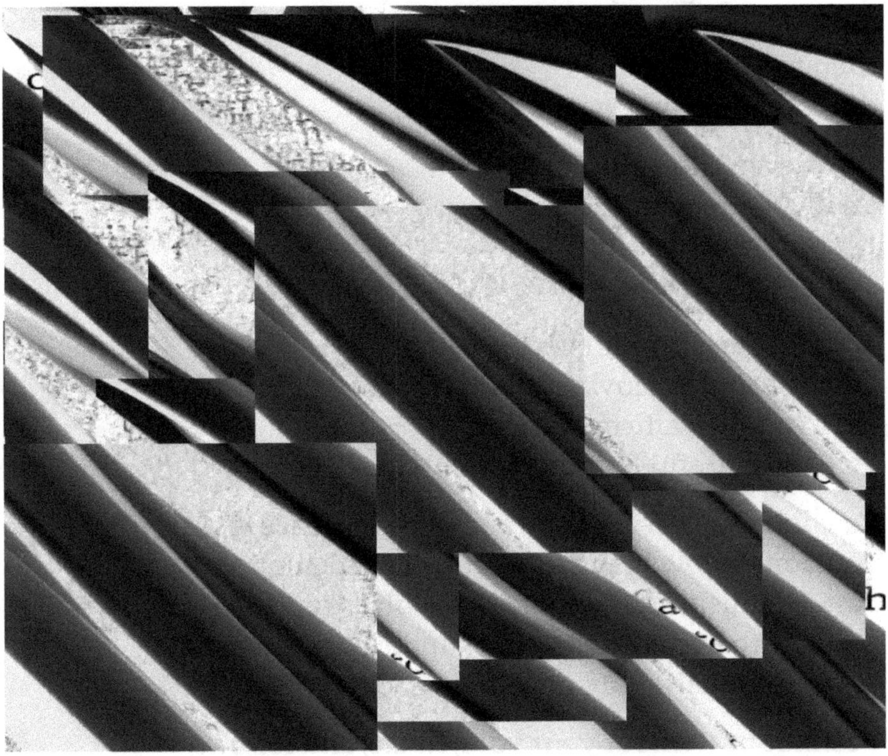

"Don't Forget the Bell"

Gimme your stars.
Please.
PLEASE!
Gimme one more star.

Don't let that finger hover,
bring it down on my star.
Tap it firm and with resolve.
Use that mouse and click.

I need it! I need it so bad!
I can't tell you how much
I've been thinking about it.
Craving your eyes on my site!

Tap all over my digital self.
Caress the page as you scan.
Flick the scroll wheel slow
then fast, fast, fast
as you speed your way to the next!

Don't even think, just click.
I will reciprocate, I promise!
I give as good as I get.
I will vote for vote.

Let me cherish your every vote.
Let me bring my loving mouth
over your life-affirming click.
I will be grateful for your support.

You don't understand the pain your absence gives!
You don't know how desperately I need another.
I am languishing without your daily attention.
I writhe to live without your support
because I am literally nothing without you!

I cannot be without your vote, heart, and follow.

Follow me to my every platform and validate
my very existence by clicking on my heart.
I need your support to justify my existence.

I'll be your digital harlot
your virtual submissive
who will take on any visage
who will act to your preference.
You need only tell me your tastes.
I will wear any wig and say
anything you tell me to say
I am that desperate to get

just
one
more
star.

Validate me by sharing my content.
Tell your friends about my poems.
Add those links to every correspondence.
If need be go that extra special length
and type out every character of my link.

I am nothing without you.
Completely and totally.
My brain is hardwired
to crave your lovely click.

I need you to complete me
by giving me online support.
I need you to reach in deep
to feel the subconscious drive
of a brain in pain from longing
that is never satisfied.

I need you to like me
,not just the click,
but to actually like me

in that parasocial way--
to worship and draw me
like one of your stream girls.

I am that desperate for the exterior.
I am so pathetically drawn to you.
You, who I don't even know;
who I honestly, kind of, don't want
to know.
I still need you to consume me
all the same because without you
--without you--
and your support
,and a purchase,
from my links in my bio,
I will only get more sad;
more empty and lifeless
and so unbelievably depressed,

because something inside me is broken.
Now I need you to treat my work like porn
because maybe then I'll be savored.
Maybe then I can actually feel like I matter,
but I know it won't work. I am broken.
I need you more than you can possibly know.

My dopamine craves the eyes of millions.
I don't care how exposed I need to be.
I will keep going far past my comfort,
debasing myself to the limits of taste,
just to feel your life-affirming star.

"end.V.3"

You're so beautiful

it makes me sick. I wanna run
up and bite your face off,
chewing on the life I've never
known. God, I can hear
your false modesty

even without the electrons separating. You
know you're a fucking gorgeous work of art
given form and I can see it in every carefully
constructed portrait you casually drop, but
you're still gonna play the part in a 1D
song, with your one dimensional
avoidance and your glib toothy shine.

I'm so fucking
jealous
of you that I'm
even jealous of your pain. It's all so new
and fresh
and vibrant
and hemorrhaging vital nutrients
and still you can blaze in the dark

like a fucking bonfire turning blood
to oil. I would rip out my insides
if it let me swap with your life
but I have a hollow interior.

I have become want.

I cry for all the glory I've never
touched, the splendor that
clings to you like failure
coalesces around my eyes. It
paints the world a shit blue

and still and still and still

I long for a beauty like yours.

Not even to own you,
not even to kiss,
not even to stand beside
and be photographed,
but to simply be you

for a year. God, a year is so big to you.
It still means something. You
don't even know how much little it'll mean when your

bones ache from sunrise to rest. I
am doing my
best to live healthy and I
can't, because of the mistakes I
made when I
first thought my
life was worthless. Now my

problems aren't choices but modalities
deep coded and you and your beauty
can be thoughtless in your moments.

Own it.

Own it all.
Be the belle
of every fucking ball because you do deserve it.
I can tell you that. I have seen so much crap
in this sanitation disposal we deem life.

I have gleamed the finest things,
the rapture, the divide. People
will kill for you. They will die
to suffer your rejection
and you hide your glory
to be a line in their fucking song.

I'm not proud of this wickedness inside, but
at least I never touched myself when you were in my mind.
At least the thought of lust is distant.
At least I am not the monster that you have to live around.
At least I am less than the salt on your ground.

I can be civil.
I will behave.
Live on as perfect.
Avoid my grave.

"Wrong Side of the Thin Line"

watching the sunrise
thinking of that thin line
between important and forgot

a twitch of discomfort
by staring at blind hope
I turn my back to that sight

I know that
nothing I've done
buys me a seat
at the golden spire,

and for all of my nothing,
I've spent all three fluids
that prove that I've arrived.
Yet I'm still pushing eighty,
driving solo on blank roads

because I can't read the signs.
Every stop ain't a pit stop but
a reminder that I'm lost.

If I sell my wheels
I might settle down
but there's
no room for me to buy,
no space to occupy,

so I drive.
It's the only thing

my hands know what to do.
What's a sun anyway?

that wavering thin line
got me thinking it's my time
but none who find success are rivals

deep in my mind palace
I can drink a gold chalice
and view the opal statues of myself

but there's no nurse to offer help
no friends to pull me out this hell
I think it's time I find a way to say goodbye

"Hanging on the Sky"

hanging on the sky
never did I like this envy
my faces you despised
but you were quoting lines of calm needs
like the weather outside
was all our fragile minds could hold still
knowing our first flight
burned the lunar sight to glow cool

how did this trick
make you sniff when all the dust was gone
down with your grift
was there a single word you wanted true
now hard bonds slipping like glue
I know this is it
but you wanted us honest
a mind hacker's promise
was kind of beyond this wreck

you ever think about the glass on the pavement
every twinkle on the black stunning as our twilight
well the crash of our lives must've left a few specks
the lights of cars upside gives our floor dance a stage
I've been crawling bloody fighting every rat for feed
I hope you're thousands of miles gone
flying past the storm's edge

but I don't wanna die alone
you said I lie
muffling down my bliss moans
but what's the big surprise
when friendless days are my norm
what can I say to conform
my bad days to your hurt
when I'm more than a mask away

I'm drifting in the sky
hoping every cloud won't start the rain
hands too wet to climb
sun a blinding sign of my shame
had you lit my night
I could've followed smoke through one chain
but on this fading life
I've gotten cold and I
keep wishing you were right
how'd you fall to glide
or did I miss you trip down a gap in the gray

I hope a tiny prick
made you cry and spit old bile's song
lost with your wish
was there a single score left in the haze
now it's so long to better days
I know this is it
but I wanted more progress
a time stellar garden
to grow the seeds of your grace

you ever think about the glass on the pavement
every cutting shard a speck broken from our windows
tell the nurses of our time keep your rhythm constant
when all the cars are upside and the stars are ghost shine
maybe up's the real lie ain't we crawling slick shadows
or will this cloud of moonbeams
end just like movies

I can't stand on white hope
or walk after black wrecks
but I don't wanna die alone

"i sry"

i saw u
i didn't try

this time

but i saw u
and i cldn't look away
i stalked
more than a little
more than i shd
i never try
hard enough to b good

but u wldn't have asked me
to b good
when we were friendly
we only laughed at mischief
and took shots for violence
don't harbor anger
for my mess

please b honest
did u look too?

do u like what you see?

have i been contrite
or does this mistake
nullify my virtue sprint

have u seen where i've been
i've tried to mimic
ur success
but i admit
ur better at being special
ur special in this hellhole
ur hellish façade caves my "so long"

i wld kill my personality
to b ur friend

again

"Mask Slip"

I let the mask slip
not fall just tilt
since ideologs saw
a world beyond restrict
asked I was blocking 80

so to save the hypo' press
I let loose a fraction
not thoughts but behaviors
expressing wrongs and nags
that couldn't be 'nored more

I dropped a score of 'haps ten
but the change in a storm
made some run for shelter
lightning teeth and thunder fits
the edge of my noxious within

so the mask's back and I pray to obsession
let the ideos talk as I reform to convention
this little crack may take time to reseal
I won't keen so you'll know it's nothing real

Mask Slip DX???

Confused? I've dissected this poem in the dissection section, explaining some of my intent on page 275.

"Jaunt in the Gray"

There's never anything wrong with me
until I'm a person that needs severing
ghosted
shunned
blocked

When the haunts come back I'm trying to heal
that mind-to-heart gash but there's no advice
except those who left were wack but all the time
I was talking to them explaining to others what
interactions we had ain't no one speakin up
about their problems then, cause it's all
sun and fame until my failing's back.

How do I learn when my guts on a blade?
What have I earned in the silence of shame?
Every honest turn is a welcome change of pace
Y'all tell me I burn like an engine in a race
But this smoking hurts that's my life in the blaze
Which phrase did I blurt to start this jaunt in the gray?

It's always nerfect pobodies or hurting crimes from me
but none that left tell me why the fuck they had to leave
so I'm bounced from one to the other extreme
til I'm raging at my patient friends about toxic positivity

and they ain't half as sick of my shit
as the person with verbal diarrhea
but they all forgive my bombs
til it's I don't wanna see ya

and society's bond means they gotta fix what bleeds
but I'm a hemorrhaging sod and no one's got the string
that they need to patch me ain't no Patch Adam's gonna
boop my nose and end an eternal suffering

cause all these leftists talking cause

and writing about fixing the world through song
but the second one autistic cog
gonna gum up their machine
they'll shoot them to a corner of vile partings
saying bye bye to the problematic
without a platform for apologies

while the same fuckers posting
about how it's sad this villain weren't given sympathies
when he a civilization murderer with aesthetics
so sick they look past injustices

and I ain't allowed to diss fictional fascists
who breed the maggots of fandom
cause they mainlining ego that says
these sad demons only need a hug and squeeze
when real monsters know precisely
how to work those same impulses
to make slaves of all of us
and they ain't got no problem smiling
everyone of them Machiavellian

our ends justify their needs
cause what they need is a bunch of sheep
who will baa at the black ones
while making shrines to the wolf's teeth

and I ain't got scars these wounds will always bleed
cause every new friend
ain't gonna tell me when to scream

we're all trained to smile white
and kick dissidents to the street
like we all one chorus singing harmony
to the ordained mouthpiece
and no matter how many soloists get social laryngitis
do we ever think mob violence
is incapable of building a better life

while the Griffith's of our world got the masses
building towers of rabble all pinned up like chattel
so their political sympathies are a leftist's wet dream
writing secret gays and runaway moms
instead of building a system that can accept
anything that steps off the party line cause we're not fine

we're a society of vacant smiles
and likes without thumbs down
cause we might get hurt to have to contort
ourselves into anything but comfort in a world
that is so far past panacea

but they don't wanna believe ya
when you tell them that political action
means votes and organizing communities
outside are real villains who know
how to soothe while they're pushing you to your knees

and all our buff bads with six packs
who love us despite our past sad
don't prepare us
for the careless dismantling
of our beliefs

but no matter what grays I display
the cultural shakers aren't phased
they want to prop up skin and surname
while they rip off those same writers
cause publishing is full of liars
and I want this corrupt chain
to break down to rusted chips but I know

ain't pobody gonna sweep up the shit
all our furnaces got one mold to continue the grift
cause we all proud of taking down Weinstein
when the next Trump comes we'll be laughing

my mask's fit tight
if I don't wanna sob I won't sigh
I'm as ineffective as a neck tie
at a long goodbye

there's a reason I don't learn knots
the last thing I need is a quick way to take off
friends and fiction keep my hands clean
but sooner or later I'll ash my world gray

"Decimal"

3.7 billion years of evolution let's me see
at night. What light that shines
doesn't come piercing, but lays down smooth
through thin brush of an untrimmed bush,
casting ambient over my ceiling and table.
I'm able to perceive shapes and if not color than shade.

4.4 million days of human ingenuity
lets my cones determine where a chip bag
is a chip bag and not a black box. Turning it over,
I store vital information in my short term
brain. Another bag from the box and I find
the same flavor. Scraping skin,
arm within, I find another.

With cookie bag in my other hand
I reach in and grab, a well won prize.
The late night snack is mine. My stomach
is already full, my mood a fickle ornery thing.
It's not about the nutrients,
but the calm they bring. It's not
in the wanting that I stuff my mouth with chips,

but in the wanting denied most frequent
some 13.9 thousand days before. I want
those salts and sugars not for their own sake
but as a reminder that my survival is not
up to fate. I want not for food nor
the nutrients I receive. What
I want is to know I don't lack

and that wanting makes me feel like a decimal.

"Last Chip"

would that I could reach into that bag
pull out the last chip gluttony demands
those crisps by the lip stop my search
they are a complete artistic design
each a bubbled structure ever preferred
to my globular mass rotten inside

without shame I can chew
and enjoy salty fat no one blames
a single taste or even a handful
I mind decisions but temperance I lack
my every grasp means to fill
my mouth entirely but even alone
I'm embarrassed to indulge

to feel the shove of matter against the back
overwhelming me to grab so much I add to the dust
that feeling is satiated I am always edged closer
so I wipe my hands, stand, and roll the bag
my time away never given chance to last

that bag of crunchy edges will soon lose flavor
oxygen is a rotting thing no clip can dispel
even in the fridge it'll pick up some smell
I've already failed at being a sublime human
my need to feed might subside if I take one more bite

with a single last chip
I can at last be done but the shape is bent
and covered in dust the promise of a bag
wasted I've only just tasted
so I wipe myself clean
and realize with some shame
the bag is lopsided and I alone can shape

by reaching in deep to eat large fists
completing innate order we all crave

is it not human to set all things right
getting up I roll that temptation tight
just before I reach the pantry I realize
this bag of shame shows my disgrace
revealing my instinct driven moment
I alone nearly finished the entire bag
there's only one way to hide the evidence
even if the dust makes me cough
even if the oil is cloying
even as the sharp edges cut my gums
I must eat it all to remove the proof of my fault

but the empty bag means nothing in the trash
when I'm in the store I think of that taste
I forget how greed makes me stuff my face
how shame keeps satisfaction away
how that lingering peak is out of reach
how I justify my every full devouring
until my feast turns bleak and gives direct suffering

and the bottom is so gross
but I forget my failure
I long for that perfect chip
if only one could fill my whole mouth
and push all my wants down

but I always pick up another bag
because the thought of being wanting
is worse than hunger reminding me
of the hunger that once consumed
my thoughts while I sat confused and lost

in school and on my feet
drinking water to stave need
so that I might return starving
demolishing every gift
to a child who ate in a race
beating rivals regardless

of the chromosomes we shared

if only every chip was as dusty
and oily and small and slicing
as the last I shove into my mouth
then I'd only have the other snacks
to kill my sleep and obliterate
my self esteem

Last Chip DX???

Read an earlier version of "Last Chip" in my dissection section, where I take a deeper look at several poems. You can find "proto Last Chip" on page 278.

"Home Remedy"

night wake
feeling afraid 'fore the hurt hits
it hits bladed
vorpal rat burrowing my bowels
running up my spine
to lacerate my stomach

water is safe

always good
always a quench to sense
dulled close to death
from a childhood reared on famine
care replacing snacks
hydration is natural
bottles avail today
don't have to endure
metallic calcium tap
swallow

be a parody of serene
trust my body's act
will reduce stress's hack
the gash feels no smaller
this night hurt
threatens to eat hours

calcium chews

devoured with extreme
measure
no calm or clever care
a desperate chomp
mocking my beastial consume
when food tried again
to fill that hole
I miss my friends

I miss trusting them
to be honest

hours struggling to sit upright
hoping digestion
will ease this along
fearing this pain's a mortar
that will wall up my youth
the last of my health ruined
as debt forces concessions
unsustainable
maintained by an undeserved love
willing to sac happiness
to squeeze out years
I will not fight for
I don't fear Death's door

bread

it works sometimes
I suffer enough to bellow "God"
a carry over from hollow hopes
learned by the screen
fostered by lonely's greed
I hate the word as it leaves
stuffing bread in its place
craving relief
wondering if sugar
will do what trauma could not

then again

it's all trauma
my mangled mind bought

"Broken Grasp"

arm broken past my severe
mangled mirror of early harm
adult in a crib left to fend
for Midas milk in glass
sucking golden light
until teen hope disappears

chest cavity hollowed to collapse
and all the pests will feast
off rigid love's audacity
to remain unbent but borrowed
whilst stains betray taboo
pleasures stolen by ego's lapse

and I reared in that hallowed ground
knew every story of the local hero
who claimed what love he had no right
yet was given to the first in splendor
like some parody of noble purpose
for lonely terror makes sponges of rocks

and I who drank from sun's gray image
sucked long on mid-day stone
memories of dew evaporate to tongue
the mist of moth's haze enveloping
eyes better suited for singing chorus
as we danced the liar's tango in rows

I sang long for Persephone
learning lyrics by tombstone's sigh
rich jugs of pomegranate drank
to celebrate her freedom gone
that bond of familial branch torn
no Spring to honor matrimony

thus my Winter preserved love's death
its corpse a statue steel and stained

my ambition what fit in a twisted hand
grasp shattered by lantern's burn
be it butane or Diego's district
my worm's view surmised
a legacy of fetid grime on carpet
a life lived hungry for Charon's ride

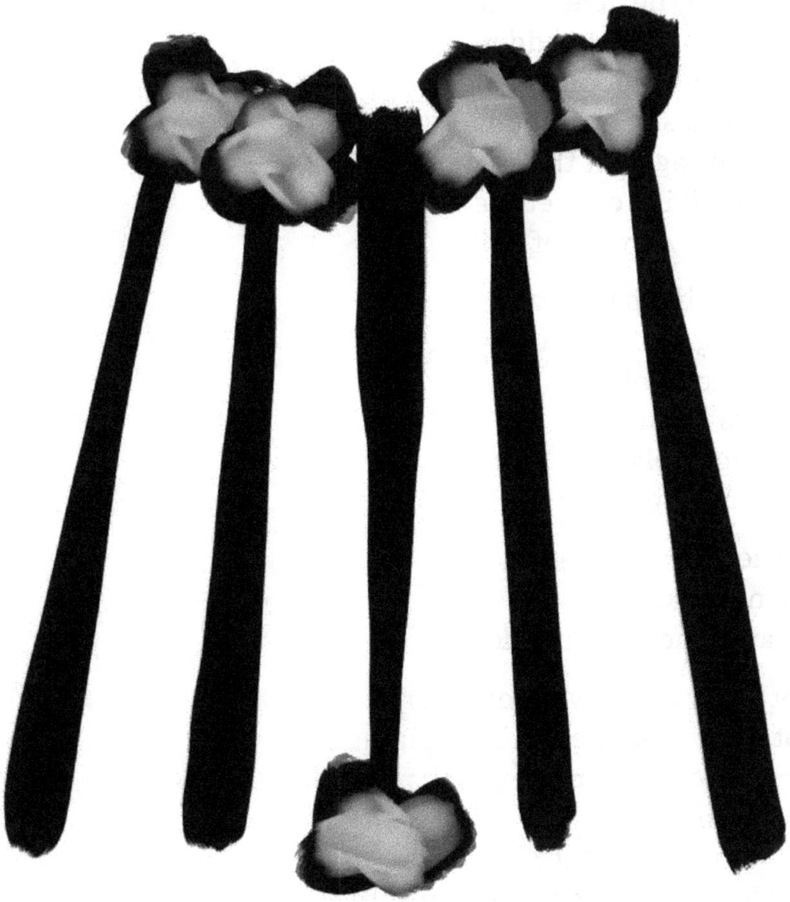

"valiant impotence"

Imagining angles
for life to drip artistically,
I trace a nail upon the swell
of tendons made thick
by a fist. It lists, my pain,

drifting ever darker,
but this ship is mine--
not yet insane.

As Eric in the maelstrom,
I turn an ancient rudder.
Among whirlpooling gales
and flashes of hurt, I put
my heart against the current.
My creativity, can set me free,
I need only dream of light.

But pushing past death's
spiraling darkness,
I have no fight.
There's no Ursula,
no dragon black,
no army of generic bad.

My heroism can be stoked,
but never keeps,
because the evil's inside me.

Not every shadow's seen clear,
not every smudge can be explained.
There are many mysteries that irrationally
trigger shame.
A door with light through the cracks.
A voice saying, "something pretty."
A vague knowledge that innocence,
gives rise to penetrating sin.

These horrors live like neighbors
in an apartment I never leave.
Up and down the stairs they wander
and if that door opens they'll flay me.

I wish I had the strength to stop them,
the will to kill them all,
but by the time I leave my corner,
the creaking stairs brings my fall.

So I can breathe and eat what my mind believes I deserve,
because the apartment of fright within me, is still haunting
when I'm safe. There is no place I can feel serenity,
only a sanctuary from the rain.

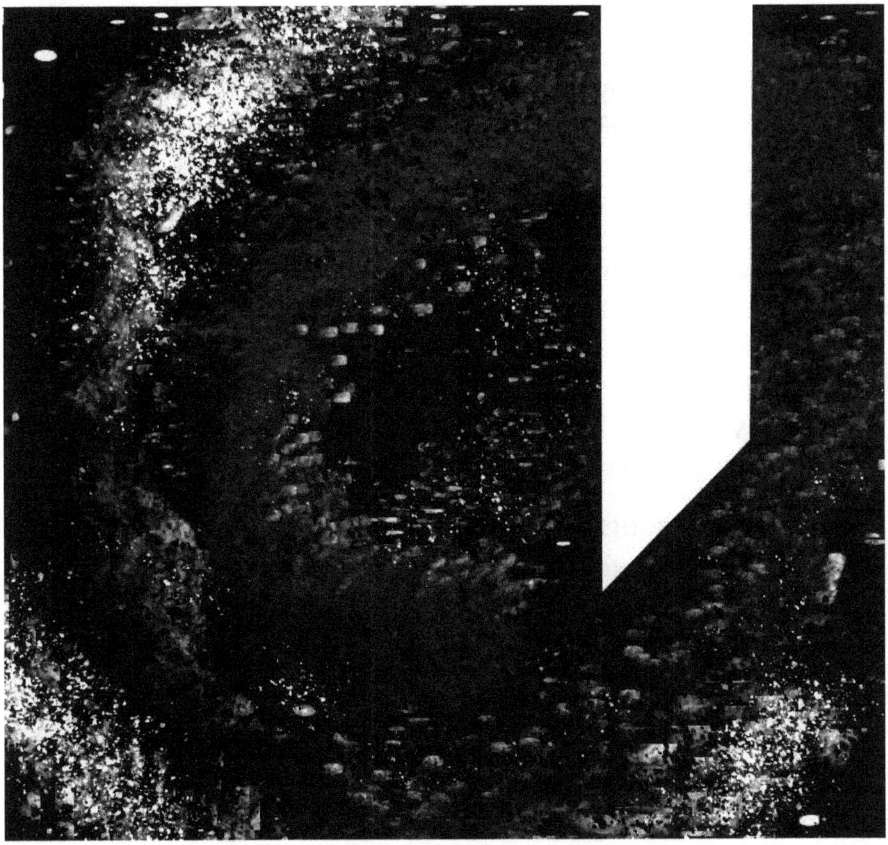

"Untitled Part 113"

I only remember accomplishments
so that I can lament what I've lost.
My gains all came with a steep cost.
My brain reconvenes all my faults
to discuss the bold third option.

I won't be defined by the drip. I can't let my convictions slip. Not for the tears. Not for my legacy, but to scoop up the wreck wrought by my smiling family. I can't let the mistakes of their sage advice take center stage in my life. I can't be the forgotten dream of a self appointed visionary who needed to rape to feel inside.

A victim's right is to keep spitting alive. I may be splitting internal but my bones are still rigid. Defined not by my trauma or the bed that they made, I have to stand tall, to step deep into the tide. If I can grit teeth and try to make waves instead of calling out a false cannonball, I will be an object worth seeing. I won't falter. I will make a splash that leaves suits ruined by bromine and monocles in their flutes.

Their ghost is gone. I'm the one haunting. I'm the one who walks the dark, my wail this nightly typing. Cause it ain't a pipe dream that I've got the drive to slice lean. Chopping that fat as I attack every last act to the satisfact' of the fat cats and the ghouls beyond me. I want the mausoleum. I want a stone bond that'll reach up and give a reason to keep living.

I want to be a song in the hearts of the dogs of this prison. I envision a world where my dropped lyrics are told from every light box they hold. To be a stellar reprieve from stories that launch brand new, old, but this narrative I gleam is a worm on a demon's string.

I chomp long, chewing on as I take my next bite. Swallow down the tallow, along with Mephistopheles's grin. That silver line within scraping my deep barrel. The tar I seal my cracks, coming off to let in the terrible. And I could laugh wicked as drops of praise make me vulnerable, to a single kick hitting like a brick as a swing on my own gallow.

My books are nothing more than compiled data files. No critic gives me a second look. I bore bibliophiles. I got no style. My substance a gross mess of thoughts juvenile. It's time to grow up. I gotta shut up and take kicks like a can on the gray mile. The pencils I push need to rub the tush of a pig slurping a nation's throw up.

The grind is clear.
Close eyes to fear.
Bleed long for dear.
My swan song ain't near.

I'm not collapsed. Get collected. Send out apps. Work my station. Be a cog. Do the job. Find a way to flee the nation. I can pick apart where they went wrong from another coast. It's better to live and suffer injustice than to be a venerable ghost.

I got a long list of grievances and twenty-five books behind me. Let the words of art die. Achieve life. Reject Plan B. The words of freedom are co-opted, they prop up a tyrant. Make a million in Amazon, and add weight to the crusher. Small press gives them money regardless. The monopoly takes their fee no matter what bodies I carve through.

I said I was a butcher, but they're packaging soylent green. I'm right there eating and "God, that's good!" At least I got meat for their pies. This heresy of artistry is making cash with blind views. They drool for cheap crap cause it churns ads the whole way through. And the best my blade can sever is the devil's line that I chew.

"past the myth"

I'll try to be
real
and let the mask
slip. It's hard
to relate the tight
fit,

but without it my mind
breaks, fragmenting
like a hand grenade,
so I gotta hold that pin.

Is it autism, vulnerable
narcissism, or just a trauma
that I let win?
I can't say.
I don't have
the brain scans or the papers

demanded to confirm
my worst suspicions,
so I keep living
with what I carry.

The scary fact about
writing
vulnerable is not
the possibility of embodying
a malignant cultural
growth,

but the knowledge
that my honest is not worth
empathy. It is the cold shame
of knowing that my worst

offenses are not behind

but instead form a line
between self
and community
that I will never breach.

So I reach out to
shake
off doubt and still the
horrors
assist in the hammering of my
fingers,

the swell in my wrist. This body
goes beyond joint deep, reaching
inside until my abused child
scowls and yells at all I create,

for my best might as well be
a negative space
defining
my anxiety
and the lies
my primitive mind is unable to dispel.

The myth making of these
confessional
poems are more ironic than
artistic,
for the fables of my
youth

went beyond those that Disney rechewed. My parents
viewed sitcoms beside me, using their terrible
examples as reason for my life to be envied. They
built no statues, but spun many yarns

and the web
around my bed
came out like

hooks
to still bleed buried
in my head.

There may one day be a way
that I will my illness to health,
but from where I write
there's only one light
and it leads straight
to Hell.

But I try to break out. I strive to let out
the emotions that are better
left buried
because I need to believe
that worship is worse
than the curse that I'm coping. I don't
hope with a breath, it takes

long

pauses

and years of reshaping my depths,
but this debt has other objectives.
It shakes off this armor I built
by every single ringlet,
sending it off like a mail,
my parts a parcel,

accruing additional fees.

I have to move on.
I need to be strong,
in every way I can.

To defend what they call wrong,
to deal myself a new hand,
but my shoulders are weary,
my mind can't find the will.

I've tried being angry,
but that fire is down to coals.
I need a new method
cause my madness won't redeem.

My new quest for self esteem must manifest.
Love is what I fight for and I will die lonely
to payback every blessing my love has given free.

Back I cast, this arcane
seal.
My lips a smooth
curl
parodying a smile
that none can relate to,
but I've gotta wear the kind
to be an exhibit in their
zoo.

"Mistaken Identity"

Do you think they really saw rhinos and thought they were unicorns?
Were manatees ever really mermaids?

I heard doves in the early morn hooting and wanted to believe that a glorious predator could exist outside my urban balcony. I saw killdeer swimming over distant lights. Their call and nightly presence convinced me that I was lucky enough to behold bats.

It was a weakness in me
To believe that I would
Witness something special
When my suffering
My poverty
My malformed cognitive processes
Were all common

I saw bats an hour before twilight feast on pests as I walked to the arcade.
I saw a barn owl not a mile from my old bed watching the grass for rabbits.
I have seen both manatee and rhinoceros bound by prisons.
We tell children they are luxurious for the animals in their zoo, but three months of isolation almost broke our society and still we pretend that an enclosure can be a comfort.

I wasn't special then
I am forgettable now
if doves can be owls
maybe I can be loved

THE MAP

"Chaparral"

life is arid in the hilly chaparral
every shade a buzzard from up high
where strange and daunting creatures dwell

what's safe or nourishing is hard to tell
a succulent might leave you withered and dry
life is arid in the hilly chaparral

the landscape a canvas of tectonic swells
each range feels close but further if you try
where strange and daunting creatures dwell

soft leaf dreams are easy to quell
knee high bushes block your stride
life is arid in the hilly chaparral

clear and loose paths mark your cell
as unseen beasts laugh at your pride
where strange and daunting creatures dwell

in the haunt of a rain that never fell
across the sky distant waves mark the divide
where strange and daunting creatures dwell
life is arid in the hilly chaparral

Chaparral DX???

This poem has an interesting structure, a form familiar for those who read a lot of poetry. Why? Read the dissection of this poem on page 239.

"I Wasn't Hurt"

I wasn't hurt.

That memory wasn't a memory at all, but a dream. That
sour itchy summer hour was a cascading irritation born
out of a forgotten cone of ice cream. My pain was
Scrooge's undigested piece of beef. That rag was
Marley's chains. I never touched a washcloth with
anything more than water on my hand. Maybe soap.
I didn't need to drop it.

Stop it.
These thoughts aren't helpful. They're delusions. They're
fabrications of a child who saw one too many books
on anatomy. Except there was pornography. I remember them
shown to his friends. Except they weren't his friends
either. He told me they were evil. They weren't worth my time
or given to sublime thoughts on morality, and
phenomena so splendidly extrasensory. I was a seed,
bursting with potential to be a fundamental part
of a new regime. Only I needed to follow his vision
to every collision with every mind too small or amoral
to connect with mine. I needed time to process what
he said, to understand that he was right and I was
braindead. That's why he always asked me about my memory,
because he knew I was too dumb to trust. My lack of lust
proved
that I lacked the cadence to explain my pain to the suits in
court
who made decisions about my fate.

It's too late to be honest.

Tell myself that the consequences were beyond
us, that I had no way of knowing what my lie would
protect. It was what's best. I was already losing
a sister and a father, did I need to lose a brother?
I don't know if he hurt her.

I don't know who I hurt by being silent. I'm beyond
this moment. I made my choice. My fib took my voice and it
wasn't a course of action I could ever take back. I am a sack
of shit that chose ignorance, only it wasn't bliss. I was remiss
in my duty to protect my sis. I am a sack
of shit who deserves a garbage fire, only guilty tears
keep justice away.
It isn't my day.

I have to wait for my body to fail.
It shouldn't be hard. I've already squeezed out
the blood of my failing heart. My morals are
empty. My mind a bad scene, written by an out
of work screenplay writer
from nineteen-eighty-three. There's a reason he was
fired and why I can't be hired.
My brain is a play with a small stage on endless replay. No
matter where the light is. No
matter who talks. I'm there on
the sidelines, singing about
my childhood gone.

Ours was a vision he made into my own.
It was no shelter but it was my home.

He took me upstairs because we were alone
and made me his lover with no words of my own.

My hand was his pencil my body his manifesto.
With each poetic flourish I tasted sour
from my end up. He wouldn't do
as I wanted so I had to compro
mise. Without the strength to
fight or led to

write my scene, I did as I was ordered
and behaved as an adult incomplete.
Never could I satisfy. Never was I right.
Never did I please him or give reason to my plight.

I was a child of trauma and an ugly one at that.
But one fact saved me, it was the heat itchy on my back.
So I promised him later
and to this day
I worry what I owe.

"Sugar Bridge I"

At the start I was smart
and I was sweet to be obedient
and brave to behave but
there's a lathe in my shame
and a crooked flame in my gut.

Your diamond gifts
are beautiful in their
mallshop round-cut
chic, but how come it's
all ruinous, and the insides
are full of shit?

A trail of gumdrops is a magical start
to a lifetime of infantilization
deading my heart. All those simps
with cavities, I'll knock their fucking
teeth free.

You think you've seen me?
You think I'm a worker bee?
I am the cog that moves backwards
and reworks your machine.

All your little head pats
fall flat. I don't need a nap
I need a scream that will bleed
all the silence binding me.
If I'm a dog, I will bite
the hand that feeds.

Your offer is awful, no matter
what treat I see. I've suffered
what you think is care, I've worked
your uniformed life of fair. I'm not scared
of a dare

and that's that.
Fuck you and your
"I know what's best for you"
crap! That why your life's
so great? That why your nights
can't find sleep? Your health

problems are adding up
like a train with no final stop.

You're a fucking joke.
Your yoke
is a rope without a knot.
I won't let it grow taught.
I won't be a tragedy
in your revisionist memory.

I don't need your perfunctory
pity.
All I ever needed was your
responsibility!

But you were too
fucking terrified
of what you'd find
on the other side
of that cyanide
mirror you preen to.

You wish you were young?
You miss having fun?
How about being a kid
who had to micromanage the shit
you let slime off your dick?

It wasn't fucking worth it!
I know, I lived it!
I was an adult before I grew up.

Out of your mouth
always comes another praise. I was cute and
reclusive, a beauty that was never
abusive. Now you're ashamed that
you know you're to blame when my
pain was plain on
every picture you forced me to take?

It's my job to build a bridge
and take down these walls?
Well, I'm building a moat of singe,
I hope you have a nice char.

"Lacking Balance"

back and forth walking on a seesaw
bending knees reacting to outside guidance
blind to the extremes but feeling likely to fall
barely hoping this won't end in violence

mocked for my lack of human defining experience
sexually charged images taunt my ego to small
pieces he mocks for being unable to come together

not caring that holes in my memory defend his innocence
he wheedles my flaws and treats me soft as a feather
for what's strong cannot be cultivated by mere indiscretions

he ridicules my bold refusal to act beyond adolescence
by treating me younger while claiming to respect concessions
but the clear choice to glory is always through horny salivating

shamed into compliance I grow bent in horror's absence
without tearful revelations my mind is pushed to graduating
thoughts of exploitation and lust though I want it none

and my outrage burns unfanned melting my face cereous
every flagellating remark expressing out towards fun
recognizing babies as dumb and every smile the sign of a liar

I grow up witch wicked and my thoughts stay ever serious
my socializing the sum of what is deemed worthy by my sire
thus with no one to conspire with I remain his loyal thrall

yet his castle is more mud than wall
the books he uses as bricks though supercilious
are all unread to add to this delirious notion
that his knowledge is an ocean I'm too weak to sprawl

but my arms work constant
and my curiosity is genuine
and my genuflecting didn't steal
my zeal for a life made clear

of the structure he did violate
so that I might never consolidate
my thoughts to realize this false God
is no more man that maggot

and I won't stand up
when I am a curious beast
made to entertain in a circus
he did conceive

but love wakes me from that dream
and though my paranoia muddles
what should be living Nirvana
I breathe in deep and ignite my rage
and burn all the wax of my face
to walk away burnt but smiling
cause no liar will determine my fate
while the puddles of my tears
reveal the shame of years

spent spinning in a web of silence
but my mouth is all teeth
burnt raw I'm ready to bleed
brutal I'll willingly end this in violence

so let him try me

"What Walked With Me"

Mine was the walk of an assassin
on a mission with a hundred
miles to go, but my canter
was no mind's shatter, I learned
the roll from being poor
and walking alone.

I walked to catch busses and so every red
was a suggestion. I walked to keep from asking
for a ride that could become taxing.
I walked when it hurt. I walked with tears
in my eyes. I walked when I was jealous
of those who passed me with contempt
and was nearly hit
by all the drivers who never checked their sides.

Missing Persons named me a nobody and I wouldn't argue
what they proclaimed. I had little purpose or import and my first
phone barely rang. Emerson said that my journey
was more important than my destination, but I lost
days and weeks walking while others were lost
in celebration.

Maybe I saw a sunset
or a cloud form
that other's missed. Maybe witnessing roadwork
I saw the city hurt
by the poorer streets
they neglect. Maybe I learned compassion by sharing concrete
with the damned,
but mostly caution
because their stink was worse when they're mad.

The roads I passed, they all last and withstood the test of time,
but the businesses are gone and my friends are hard to find.

Behind a cemetery a tall green fence marked my path to school
for four years of sorrow and two with a smile. It was behind
the dead when clouds grew bitter, I got wet, but I resolved not
to be sick and my constitution bared it.

A few more blocks, with soaking socks, I passed a friend
of a friend who once asked if anything I said was true,
and I was too smashed to tilt back to the platform.
Stepping away from Brawl, I felt a fool.

Along the same road, I hitched a ride,
from a gay friend who liked to taunt
me by twisting his tongue in three languages,
when I was a change in his business.

Every road comes with a story
but the concrete gave no glory,
only reasons to wallow.
I learned
to stop the burn
of my stomach with a swallow

of water. It only got worse when I grew older. For a kid
with frayed jeans and holey shoes might draw
sympathetic views, but an adult was a lost
cause, no reason to stop
and offer a ride to a near stranger.

Though there might be a slightly great
appreciation for infrastructure in me,
I found the destination touched me,
even while I was on my feet.

For on my way to taste my fate, when best friend
punched my face, the sky was grim and muggy
and on the return it was clear and lovely. And on
those nights when I was young and mumbled songs
of unrequited love, the moon was soft and misty,

because I'd seen her crow's feet.

Another path
I took fast because I missed my friend's laugh.
Another shortcut
on the railside gave me dreams of my sweet demise.
Another day,
another week,
I kept going down the same street,
and when I couldn't,
those roads were quiet,
because I knew my soul was violent.

Now my walks aren't the same and I don't miss them at all.
My weakness grew with my waist, but at least I stand tall.
In the whole of my life those walks gave space to picture:
unworthy lovers, magic spears, sword fights, dragon riders,
and dark nights where somehow love and hope conquered all.

"Sugar Bridge II"

Kids grow up so fast --

when you don't supervise them,
and they have to raise each other;
getting in fights to settle disputes;
violating rights in abusive discovery.

At five, maybe three, my test
a ceremony of age, unasked.
Forced to play adult by shame,
brother gave a failing grade
but a slimy chance to retake.

That shake...
I shook.
I took all I had to.
Came away fog brained
but resolved to have no
feeling or drive. No
desire to deny. No
hope entertained.

From one statistic to another.
I, a victim, cyclical abuse,
thee that hurts shall ruin together.
My fate, to rape, as I was used.
To save the next face,
to stop the next stage,
I shut off tears and smiles,
but couldn't stop my wild

fury. Like a roach I was full scurry.
A scary enemy of any kid who tried
befriending me. All the teachers seen
what they seen, wrote me off as a bad
scream. But they talked on about "soft

paws, gives hugs instead of fists" not
giving a shit that my autistic distance
might be more than unfound divergence.
I made them nervous so they turned
a bind eye to every bully and tear cried.

Now, all the little kiddies
need to sit in the big circle;

not too close, you might touch
a knee or dress or spread
the disease of your fucked
up way of thinking. Shithead.

Time to sing about kindness.

Regardless of whether any guardian
has the stones to stand against
the criticism that will crash on them
for pointing out that a problem child
is a textbook sign of heart death.

Talk about sharing,
learn about caring!

Ignoring habitual isolation as a sign
because my personality has to be shy.
No room to conceptualize battered reality.
They have to sanitize Earth to be rated
all ages, so I guess my rape happened
during commercials.

Rehearsals for buddy bonding.
Show those cuties. Share gifts,

with a kid they'd sooner kick
if they weren't performing smiles.

Don't build walls,
build up a bridge!

All their sweet platitudes,
never changed an attitude,
never raised a portcullis,
but gave stipends to corrupt
admins selling futures for cars.

Where's our bridges?
They melted like candy,
sugar high in a ditch,
those who couldn't lie
knew their chocolate was shit.

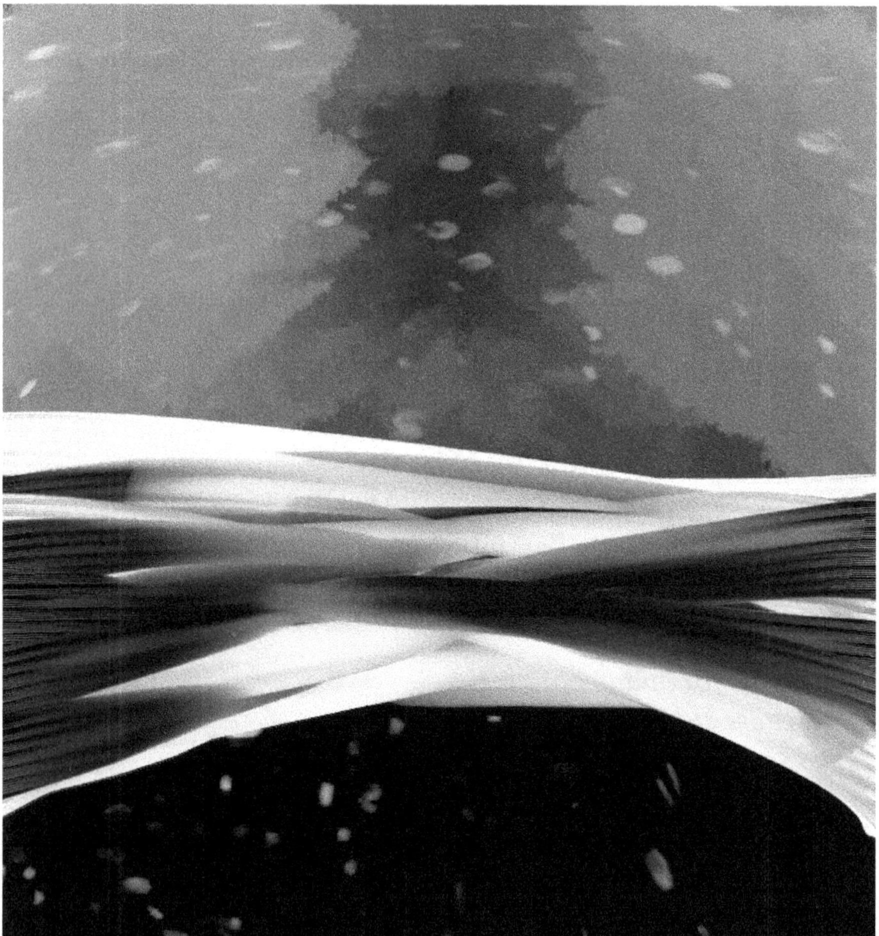

"Backfist"

Fear fighting.
A tear lighting,
the shimmerin's in the way,
every lampost a new haze.
In my squint eyes
that never see right.
Even when the threats all alone
I had a fist ready to bleed
and a grit that was all me.

I got my scowl right.
I had my fist tight.
I was dirty fucker few liked
with a death glare
that saw through right,
and the bitterness
I held kept the tenderness impaled.

See it wasn't summer, but it was fucking hot cause the smog wasn't choking up the cogs and so we took it. Everyone one of us sub-four, had to cough and take a tour of the worse they had in store. But the blind were right cause they only saw the scene of the playground and their friends and the cartoons on TV.

I was stumbling. I was fading. I had a foot
in the grave cause I knew an angel wouldn't save
a little fucker worse than a knave. I wasn't special;
weren't George Bailey. I didn't have friends
to keep me happy or a community I saved;
I was worse than a knave.

Some might call me brave but I weren't a friend
to the end or even for a minute. Every smile
was a lie and I saw the pity in it. It was hot,

but it wasn't summer.

I was churning memories that festered,
knowing my life was shit now,
but I stood to inherit a world of cow
chips. And with a chip on my shoulder
my smolder turned colder.
My mood went dark
and my brood became a river

on a face that resented every phrase in my mind
I couldn't hide
couldn't separate the pain
from the now
and the then
and the when
that I spent all my days
growing cold and afraid
cuz the humans that came
before prophesized
a dominion of pain.

And they saw me. Twenty maybe forty kids,
all put eyes on me. And their sympathy.
Their fake fucking tears for a shit they'd ignored
for a year, was falling on a grass drier than the asscakes
in the pisser. Yeah, I was bitter. I knew once I went back
to moping they'd all go back to hoping I stayed
far from their games and never said their names.

So I ran.

I ran from half my grade and ended up in kindergarten's
land, but one caught me. And he stopped me. And he
asked about my pain and with shame I let it rain. And in
that moment, though I knowed it wasn't anything
to last, he acted like I wasn't last in their thoughts
or their prayers, but the thing is that sympathy
runs drier than a well that led me straight to hell.

Another day,
I couldn't pay for a meal and I lost
my composure in a corner.
Of the cafeteria stalls I didn't think
that my falls would cost me so much,
or that my pride could be crunched.

So since I failed to do my duty as person
and a student at that school, I walked away
hungry with hate. And there was a boy

that was my friend
but since every enemy
looked like a friend,
I thought him simple.
Bro told me he was abysmal.
So he and his bud saw the mud
that squelched beneath my feet
and showed me sympathy.
I didn't want that pity.

Fear fighting.
Teeth grinding.
I had my fist tight
and the march right.
But this fucker
wanted to help and he grabbed me and asked what's my hell?

and I threw back
like a badass
and his nose went crack.
See I acted like that monkey,
but I knew I was striking
like Bruce Lee. I made him bleed.

But the act was so fast and my escape
was beyond crass. I didn't even look
back and my rage and my blurred

sight kept me from feeling
when my backhand hit his feelings.
So I kept walking and I kept brooding.

When they found me
and took me to the office
for exerting violence
I didn't know which
mistake I'd made.
After the lectures and the calls
and robbing hours from my mom,
I found he wasn't mad.
Like a hero he wondered
if I was still sad.
And I cried and hid my face
and never once spoke
the way that I felt
to a boy that had a true self.
Cuz I was pure trash.
I was lower than low and

worse than a knave
I hadn't a heart worth love
or a spirit to save.
I was flesh that lived on
but a mind too dumb
to be anything I dreamed.
I was ever dead it seemed
and I was trembling at the

thought
that my life
wouldn't end.

"No Place for Smoke"

one
spark
searching for old furniture

lone
mote
riding light of honest heat

web
grown
twisted loose by hornet beat

quake
the rattle of a house hungry for murder

slam
the door before anyone push carnage
I was beyond any solipsistic insight
what world was bared were the teeth
impairing even partial relief amygdallic fight
never gone to night so my cage was the day
of living in screamless pain cloaked as love beams

sun
beam
following cold bird's timeline

wild
beast
too full to puncture veins red

roach
dream
indisting' from hard spring bed

feast
on grudges while we sharpening our teeth white

paint
the blame any shade but the right of CPS's tape
but under lying decay curls it down to woodgrain

poked feet on nails while I hopped over feces
kicked termite sod and hum out they baby
cause this inner God got a long way to crawl

'fore I gave hope another shot and in that chaos cradle
neighbors gave odds to another short shout or the third
police call but every bawling inner dying was a triptych
rhyming family with ennui and the tragedy of twenty years
of lost dreams but they spun a good yarn from tears crystalized
food stamps denied while we picking fights for lunch rights

and from all their myths
and their dark dances
not one of us would
give life another chance

down
play
the screams sounding every loss

talk
up
a bond stronger than sitcom

hug
back
every night without father

be
parent to mother and friend to Dad
learn the smoker's cough
and keep the spark a glowing ember
let the wood burn
till my bones are charred evil

keep
fire
hot until I birth the sequel

"Muddy Crush"

Accused of an absence a lack of witnesses
bolstered claims of my supposed crime.
I, the only suspect, formed a lineup of one.

The constable, my fretting mom,
whose anxiety attended to play bad cop.
The detectives worked to lessen sentences
for good behavior. With one exception.

She came forth from civic halls to volunteer
her services. Cause she alone had the stones
to declare herself an expert of facial expressions.

My judge walked past metaphorical glass
dividing suspects from authority. That direct
path even came past the barrier of sensibility.
Another step and I was close enough to smell
of more than guilt. I worried terribly

about a stink because schoolyard students
once told me that an odor hung upon me,
but I was quickly beyond the ever-present trembling
of never-welcomed memories. This figure

whomst I had never before met
was just then inches apart to play expert
and her opinions came with scrutinizing
eyes that hoped to yank out my brain
and dissect what was mine. I lost all time.

She wasn't sweet.
She wasn't kind.
I, the miserable suspect,
was a mere insect to divide.
She, like a mystic,
used my face to divine
some altered state

or the waylay signs
of a deception devised.
I stood still as an obedient dog
and she bid me to bark.

What words I said,
I could not find.
For they did little to
mask what was inside.
This vision of justice
was more than I
ever thought would
come close to
a loser such as I.

Though buried,
my heart hurt to beat.
Pumping up fluids
to a surface dry
but my soil cracked
and she made mud
of the feelings I denied.

I was crushed
by most dangerous
biological functions
I couldn't even reckon
so her every inflection
brought a red to cheeks
that she couldn't help

but think was a sign of guilt, and if asked I knew damn well
I was guilty, only not the absence I no longer cared to defend.
So laughing, half mad from tortured stammering, I repeated
my innocence to the expert who then stepped back to speak

of me, to the constable and her minions that were my siblings.
My guilt was an uncertain thing, but I would be punished

with constant lecturing. That fate I couldn't even hate,
because that whole way back my brain hung on
to the only sanctuary it knew, to tell myself she was too

old to see me as anything but a child lying to save my hide.
But our heights were roughly the same and her grace marked
a place reserved for only perverts and the deranged.
Had I seen her again, maybe her beauty's spark would've
lit the oil clogging my heart, but suffocating reality

let me
run back
to hide
in that
dark pit
where
lust died

"Gutter Boy"

Drawn to an angel,
boy from the gutter.
Weeping for a savior,
kept by my brother.
Cain to his Able,
loved but unwanted.
Searching for the angle
to clear my hauntings,

but no matter how the book cracked,
no pages offered filled what I lacked.
The treasure in his mind was always
dark once I tried to peak.

So a cross quartered my sky.
Simple light,
blinding true
from the worm's eye.
My soul's filth
fertilizer
for a garden divine.

Away from what I lacked
rejected from his sacc.
It sufficed to know that
beauty shone
beyond his demands,

but that Eden
wasn't flush with kind
or even sunshine.
The boys spoke hate
and joked of rape
while memorizing
God's lines.

Without invitation or handshake,

I dared not follow the steps
their friendships asked I take,
but with caped justice
my eyes watched every girl
who joined their darkened sides.

Yet the bell of service
rang
and I left
a girl with hard eyes
to her fate
with that boy's hand
on her back
not a glance
given
to those out back,

and in the sobering threat
of a joke or a dare or a scare
or a poke,
I kept repressed memories
of rape close,
as the conmen
climbed the stage

and used a magician's charm
as proof of God's long arm.
Evil's avatar, a telephone book,
ripped by a strongman's yoked
physique, but teen cheers lied.
They voiced the same fake
enthusiasm a schoolside
chocolate sale made.

No figures lingered
in the far tree's shade.
That girl's fate,
if at all dark,

I could not say,
while looking my ride
asked if I was okay,

and knowing my concern
was born from dropped eaves
I left the shadows to grow
on the coming of eve.
"No," settled fears
and I left church
with strangers.

I ranged the spiritual plains
hoping a scorpion sting
could inject some sense
into a boy lost in dark dreams.
Between an abuser's myth
and the pedagogues grift,
I wandered in stolen minutes
my mind purchasing a ticket
to leave the terrestrial hell
and seek a luxurious cell.

Yet, the God I touched was no prime creator.
That capital He a clergy's greed made savior.
I felt their need, their conspiratorial web
a trap of biblical lines weaponized by death.
So I followed not that glowing offer of numb
and looked no further for salvation or fun.

Having conquered Christian hope
I awoke to no bright truth
instead bound to live
in a prison frozen by youth
and the heat of shame
nor the debt I held as blame

gave me the force to shatter

that curse. Misanthropy
and nihilism
and rejected thoughts
of hedonism
brought me back
to that old familiar
comfort
of a grave dug and filled
by my own hand.

From the gutter
to the sewer
I could only hope
my manure
would give life
from the sutures
my mind
never supplied.

ROAD TO MALTHENA

1

you were my first
i was your pest
in jest you were a Goddess
i bent low in service
you claimed the crown of evil
i shivered to receive your cruel

Limerence had me. I wasn't bad but I'd been
nothing that was good when your smile found me.
An instant of weakness became a pattern
to distress you, when life already made you slattern.
No reason to trust, regardless, you gave it thus,
but I, in my lust, romanced you like forgotten gum.

Hear my sticky tale, oh, spirit of love gone pale!
My devotions were a flood of emotions,
broken past a damn of incoherent justifications,
for life lived mellow, with an inert heart inside.
My crimes, felt sublime! My every trespass
came with no news flash that I was Einstein,
nor even a Casanova, but an extra that didn't last
past the director's first casting call. Such was my fall.

See too that this prechewed narrative may be apparent
that it's stale flavor doesn't warrant, a long list of warnings.
For the dirge of my folly was short but oft sung, and I learned
from the churn of my guilt and a stab to the hilt by that beauty
I did love. And my blood formed no scab, for my wound
I would not scrub. That infection left me breathless,
my every friend saw the pus and smelled my putrid
want for a heart that deserved the service of her pure bliss.

Yet limerence burns brighter than Gatsby's green star.
For every broken secret cries in agony to be heard.
Though the bands play it daily and the actors know these words
before the scripts are passed en masse, or the typing of a writer.
It is a blinding, wretched thing that calls the hopeful to the depths
and I nor anyone can deny that yearning that defines acceptance.

my story was not first
your horror was truly worse
than my palpitating anguish
for your haunting that I languished
my hand sought your crown of evil
your mirror caught my psyche's tendril

2

you were my first
i was your friend
a safe harbor for me to spend
my days in genial ardor
you claimed the crown of evil
i attended court thinking us equal

Love was lost. Made spectral by a scrutinizing host
in my brainpan, so I couldn't stand to hear the hopeful
squabble like birds. You, in your grace, attended my concerns
like a cook using the books I burned to smoke your meat.
I was fed your dish with a season of good reason and a garnish
of nobble wisdom to taste, but lo, I was still ace.

Under the light of dim stars, we met, and when I left with a shrug
dramatic, you panicked, and picked up your verge.
For I had no right to dare to abscond without leave,
so an earthen clad seneschal was sent to bring me to my knees.
Apologizing for the insult, my dissidence I vowed to purge.
Abysmal thoughts were spinning my being like a drug
anyway. Any day my intransigence caused despair,
gave cause to dislodge my indolent cognizance.

Yet that specter was no feature of a mind grown to lag,
but a creature made evil at a sunny day in bed.
A dagger of shame given to me,
made sharp by lies of mockery,

a skinny blade shaved down to memory,
that punctured my humanity.

And lo, I was twisted to a form resembling the natural.
And lo, my sweaty disgust was actual.
Not a nightmare I'd survived,
but a terror I'd find
anytime that my eyes
took in the morning sunrise.
And my stomach got sick
And my reason felt thick
from a monster's wicked
sweaty ill-fated trick.

Then,
upon the horizon between life and death,
came a visitor with orange fur, her head an elephant.
Then,
lowering one paw, she bowed deeply and called
me to climb upon her shiny coat and ride back home.

On a ride of clouds past balconies,
where termites feasted for centuries,
the baku swam gently to hades.
Stepping off scared, I got to the shore,
and walked into darkness where no sound could form.
The winged brother of living death
shook my hand firm and I drank from Lethe.
Didn't He at least see me,
struggling to breathe?!

3

you were my first
i was your pest
a chittering contrarian
souring your midnight
you claimed the crown of evil
and i yearned for a sequel

Trust was frost. No summer ever pierced the haze
of her opal shawl of single minded devotion
to a scream that echoed back from the ocean,
rolling rampant against stagnant unrealized dreams.

For a woman made a girl by the infantilizing eyes
of those that sought to shelter a beauty from her fervor.

I knew not to how to serve her, for you in your opal shawl felt more amber
than gold or garnet. Yet you were hardened, made tough by a conviction
that I only ever glimpsed but could never press my void-thick obsidian
into a key hole sealed by caution quite reasonable. See the bees of my
weak knees were more sting than pollinating being. It wasn't my honesty
that pushed you from me, but being candid there were stagnant dreams
that hadn't soil to water then grow to shatter glass ceiling and patriarchal
discipline that kept your feelings hidden lest you be named bad.

I think we all build Floyd's wall, though my surrealist prison was more pit
than confining isolation. Yours was all yours and where I touched it was
cold.
I never wanted to shatter but my patience couldn't handle climbing
when you sang like Rapunzel with a casual lob. So your every smile
pushed back my want for a while and your scorn burned my yearning
desire for a friend who'd survive the trial of my psyche, collapsing violently.
With all this between us I'd say I did my best; thought your tower ivory
was but a place to rest. Not knowing Hypnos held my spirit.

That shake,
when a child made a deal in the depths of hades,
I knew not what he'd conceal in my heart of hate.
That shake,
from the baku to the shore of darkness,
swore me to seek bliss through ignorance.

Others might've seen what was growing in-between
our hearts.
From a midnight balcony like a Shakespeare scene
our hearts
formed a bridge that surpassed all we'd build to protect
our hearts!

So we wandered in our dreams, finding comfort, hearing things
that every cricket of celestial destiny could sing!
You slept between nights wept for thee!

I accept that these
stirrings might just be
the passing breeze

of a mind digesting we,

but my deal with Hypnos blocked my path!
Our meeting in slumber went askew so fast!
You heard a voice familiar and with courage asked,

"Oh, kind spirit
have you heard it
in the pages of fate
who I might long to date?"
And without shame
that spirit gave my name!

4

you were my first
i was your pest
but lost in honest
longing freed by rest
you dreamt of fate
i tumbled violent

Into Lethe. I spent my creeping dread borne sweaty from violation
made permanent on that scrunched up bed. Haunted forever,
instead, I traded heart's character for Hypnos's great paradox.
Though I forgot how, He marked my mien, taking baku pelt
and spreading felt and orange fur into my childish face.
As putrid puberty made a pervert of me, the gold and rust hex
did vex my every sleep. In dreams of death, He gorged upon suffering.

Through the bond of dim stars, you called. Using magicks blocked
by Hypnos's hand, I was bidden to your sanctuary's land. Yet the mists
of slumber's kiss were no longer mine to soar. No baku's back
lent for that poor child who ignored his every flicker of heart's
passionate purpose and so their service lacked. I, the scruffy teen,
only just thrice annually marked with baku's shade,
did walk on groundless aeons and fell victim to the thousand sirens.
No rocks broke my keel, no shores dashed my skull,

but verily,
I did easily
forget the life
that was my own.

There are no rhymes of Abendell
for most minds never touch it.
This place in mists gives lives a twist
and changes fate for promise.
A child may sleep but for a day
and wake with a father's experience.

Inside its halls, life breathes, objects fall,
and all of existence behaves obedient.
For this place in dream where baku dwell
is no less real within. All that eat have to
stay until time pulls back its curtain.
Yes, a life can be lived in just one stint
in Abendell's foul illusion.

I questioned not how I awoke attending a new school.
The roads were clean, the town closed in by dark woods
cloaked in sunshine. That wall of pines seemed pure divine
and every student spoke to me with patience.
This school, the change, I found it strange, but accepted my life anew.
For every grade can feel insane as the student body shifts around you.
I studied long, I shaved my face, not knowing the hex still pricked my skin.
Though my journey started to meet your sanctum, I found your echo within.

She was kind and shy, mischievously clever and quick of mind.
Her hair was raven, her skin sunshine on the sand-worn rocks where you stood tall and screamed for all the injustices you survived.
Yet this glorious woman, she was just as uncertain as your vision, I surmised.
Through that trick of dreams, I could not think, of whom this teen reminded me.
We were of an age, and with youthful esteem we established camaraderie.
A month did pass, and two more still, and I spent afternoons escorting her home.
She welcomed me and, joyously, I ate more than Persephone.

My friendship felt stable and she had not your able
bodied guards standing around on high alert.
She took my hand without love's demand
and shared thoughts below the surface.
In misery my heart did bleed to view her precious smile.
For the time I lied about my insides, she spake no hurt a-purpose.
I and she knew sweet symmetry, until my closed heart grew hostile.

Some simple spat mirrored that feast you served with wisdom most nobble.

Lo,
in waking life,
I could not find
a sensation of pained longing.
Lo,
in dream's divine
precious experiment, my time
gave name to my heart's spurning.

With supercilious disdain,
I approached your dream-formed shade.
Angry for feeling so much pain
I took her arm serious and spake
those words that gave physicality to dreams.

And I woke shivering and half dead
my alarm clock blaring
I was past late and fled
without shower, without care for teeth,
I made a mad dash upon that street
and the cold and cruel reality
kept my broken heart from lingering
on the woman of my dreams
that coincidentally
reminded me

of you.

Class attended.
Bus ridden.
I stepped off
and scoffed
as the spell
of Abendell
turned my wall
into a ladder!

Out that pit,
I climbed the summit
and cried the tears
of a heart

saved by
your twilight.

5

you were my first
i was your pest
in jest you were a Goddess

too many times over
too many lines i
struggled to find a
reason your sublime
declaration spake
true to my heart's want

For in those earliest days, drunk on Lethe's haze, your quavering
beauty required an explanation that consistently eluded me.
Of what possible reason could some lonely boy feel drawn
to a declaration of divine providence requiring regal song?
Denied lust was made rust from the tears I could not shed
and for every palpitation you gripped startled within your chest
mine pained me thrice more before your celestial bridge
gave me passage to Abendell's lovely delusions.

That mirth most rare that did gleam between your skin so fair
gave more reason than the seasons of my perverse wants left to simmer.
Blinded in the radiance of your smile, I did long to share
in this joke that your presence was made permanent by ambrosia.
So I bowed serene before my transgressions ever gave your
seneschal cause to lay out misgivings for my odd departure under dim stars.
Yet my worship granted no title of service, no list of tasks to please thee.
Thus my confusion gave no conclusion to a hidden masochist's fantasy.

I understood not what feeling that crown of femininity had wrought
upon the head of a woman repressed by dread that her heart's wants
would surely have brought ostracizing consequences to a lady lacking station.
Your destiny was headed for damnation and so what God given right
did your life's night foretell but to be shamed in public and sent to divine gaol.
Under such circumstances, you had to decide your blood was colored evil.

And no,
I know not what sequel
your glorious design
made of the love
you contrived.

Yet,
I felt your jest
was always more
than a trifling
thing

thrown about
while we
wandered around
your lovely
aura.

But the feelings of empaths don't last beyond the song of a trauma stricken traveler.
Yet to move on would be wrong whilst spinning the narrative of my Spring's surrender.
You were a God because that was wrong and that too added credence to your wicked splendor.
I sensed a fog covering skeletons forgot in that tower ivory and its cerebral equivalent.
Know that it came to me in seconds to bow and worship at your feet because my diligence
was more than kink hidden, but a longing to show you that your divergence was brilliant.
Though you made no effort to explain your presence as both godly and psychopathy,
I enjoyed the game of service not half as much as the promise of getting to know thee.

And here at last we come to the begin,
to explain a title more nobble than origin.
For your inspiration laid guarded like lust
and all my pining never garnered trust.

So like Zeus you did conceive a Goddess:
a glorious strigine conqueror known for olives,
the wisest and strongest of all on Olympus.

No other divine being ever seemed equivalent.

Made evil by secrets,
and kept firm in thy head.
You were Her birth
and Her being
and the prison she shed.
The Goddess of all things-
Malthena,
My Darkness.

6

I think we all build Floyd's wall,

mine more pit than confining isolation.
You reached across Malthena's prison
and pulled me out of mine.

By Hypnos's hex I missed your bridge
and slept in a land beyond time.
I met your echo in Abendell's foul illusion
and at last digested nobble wisdom
to learn the name of my heart's spurning
and break the walls of my psyche's prison.

I knew at last the truth I denied.
Out that pit, I climbed the summit
and cried tears of a heart
saved by your twilight.

Yet for all my anguish my growth could not start.
Like the bird who knew only a cage I stayed
in that pit where my wall gave a space to crawl
cause my psyche thought love a fancy born
from all the disgust churning in my forlorn burn.
I had no salve or an ephemeral lamp to shine
my despair was mine, finely crafted to never
once be adapted into something I might sever.

So in my ignorance, I spoke freely of a life unwished
by the scathing defenses I built to reject love's
advances, because it wasn't sex I feared but violation
of my right by those I trusted with my vulnerability.

What treasons I suffered I neither conceptualized
nor were memories criticized, for I was blind
to the betrayal by my deal with Hypnos. You follow?

That hollow depth in my chest
was finally waking from its death.
In Abendell, I caught a drop
of that hydration that promised
to jolt my my heart's clock;
for my spirit wasn't wannest.

I looked to love not with fear but with hope and wonder
cause the joy others shared might by mine to savor.
No more did I labor under the specter of a sweaty day.
I saw my future shared with another like that kind shade.
But my training was debilitating, sapping me of mind's great
gift: to imagine what could be where there isn't. Consequently,
though I searched for her memory, I didn't see you. Honest.

Lo,
in waking life,
I could not find
the mirror of your splendor.
Lo,
in dreams divine
precious experiences, my time
was wasted on stubborn yearning.

The time that passed,
I'm sure you'd laugh,
was the same three
months I lost drifting
in Abendell's foul illusion.
With no conclusion,
no sign of your echo,
I spent a ride with you.

We were in the back,
both tired and baked
from a sun happy,
and a friendship
half strained by
withering jealousy-

for one I envied
and one I thought,
in all honesty, that
you probably had
feelings you secreted,
in that half spoken
argument's odor,
where I tried to push
your feelings to candor,
in the dusty sunset,
beside your earthy
seneschal--I trusted,
with no awareness,
I laid my palms up
and expected slaps.

Instead
you took
my hand

dragging
me out
of that
pit by
jumpstarting
a heart that
was never dead but full of a life
brimming with passion for you.

As our fingers intertwined I died inside
and phoenixed into a myth that felt right.
I would've at least been prepared to reject
a simple kiss, but that was so intimate
that nothing in my worries prepared me
for a love that swallowed every protest.

It was love
undeniably
and I was
gripped by
sharp silence.

7

My love for you
was like the bloom
of a million locust eggs
laid in the deepest
driest
desert.

It was slow to wake,
needing months to grow
and mature into anything
more than a shy grub
that feasted on everything around,

but once it did a startling metamorphosis took me.
I changed. I got big with ambition. My eyes became red,
seeing love and your reflections in the spindle of

every beam of light,
every mote of dust,
and every cloud
in every sky

seemed shaped by your memory,
reminding me that you existed
in the world and beyond all reason
you found a way to show me
not only kindness,
but physical intimacy.

In my metamorphosis
I knew one purpose
and I pursued love
with that same blind
ambition of a locust
searching for a meal. For your existence
was the rainstorm of a lifetime,

a wonderous impossible thing
that made every soul wake up
and realize that drought
was not a suitable persistence,
but a thing that the dying endure
because they have only known suffering.

Your presence was that kind of phenomenon

that reworked the world around you
and yet somehow beyond all reason
you lived in isolation seemingly
afraid of your own splendor.

I had no lack of nourishment
to find in your wake
but it was never once what I craved.
I devoured tales of you
and left fertile fields in ruin
as the shifting winds promised
that your scent was a life giving
sanctuary that would end my
need to eat until I collapsed.

I could settle down
in a place without want.

Yet, everywhere I flew,
brought me no closer to you.
With each ruining of your blessing,
I made a fool of myself, presenting
me as a clueless sap consumed
by lack of feeling, but too blinded
by pain to stop and reflect
on the secrecy you deserved,

and so like that plague
that only comes once in a generation,
I fed from the opinion of every person
in my life, leaving no room for speculation
on how I felt about you. So even though
I had only spent one week in brutal,
ravenous want of your memory,

you knew how I felt even before I talked to you,
and my plans for a beachside confession,
became a gathering of friends too large
to give us our time alone. Had I any sense
of the devastation I'd already wrought,
of the embarrassing things I had asked

and confessed, I would've let you return
to that tower ivory, but instead I told a friend
that I would stay and confess that very night.

My impatience wasn't born out of anything like
a need for honesty, but out of a pained desperation
to stop this hemorrhaging of feeling,
to know if my desires could be woven
into a blanket that warmed us in the coldest nights,
or if my spasming heart was the prelude to dying
that had no promise for another life.

My love for you was more
than a plague on our reputations
and the patience of those around us
for it ate away at me with caloric demands
far beyond the flight and feeding
of my now singular existence.
I was a thin quivering thing inside

and your presence was a calming trickling
compared to the accelerated starvation
I suffered in your absence.

You knew why I stayed behind
and with courage and compassion
you made no effort to dispel my drive.

Had I any thought beyond you
and the pain in my chest
I would've begged for us
to walk to a place where
your family couldn't hear us.
Instead, I followed you
to that square of concrete

and we talked.

8

there were no mems sharing our seat
i thank you for that
no deceptive tone or cliches repeat
i thank you for that

past the hour our bodies craved peace
sorrys are past due
my theatrics ensured a future audience
sorrys are past due

had we not started with my self deception
i was lovesick daft
contrasted horribly with your coronation
you were right to shoo
if only i admitted my feelings after that ride
i was lovesick daft
if only you heeded dreams cherished inside
you were right to shoo

perhaps our love could've been discovered together
not scraped out of secrets from some hackneyed drama
but felt in their sincerity and named our soul's tether
not suggested to be a mistake of sinful biology
our feelings could've shaped an enduring foundation
instead of laying rotting rocks towards my fetid dharma
we could've been we regardless of any observation
instead one talk added reasons for apology

i did my best to be forthright and disimpassioned
to make it clear that my lust would never harm
i gave reasons for sensations that perplex language
instead of expressing the languish cause by your lack
i explained my trip to Abendell omitting the best
that in your presence my love gave me a true home

you told me of your dreams where spirits whispered
how the clue could only be the fool beside you
you relayed with dismay how your seneschal was discussed
how I voiced with worry that my love was a bloated crush
you were patient and kind prepared to let me weep
no matter how much it hurt that your side was rehearsed

and we played out our talk of memories and conversations we shared with anyone but the only parties our discussion should've dared to include but you knew too much and I confessed too little you were bold and unblushed
and I scared to be in your circle
yet somehow
despite this

you reached out
and grabbed
my hand
to recreate
that moment
that damned
my heart to years of regret
for in that confession
in that interlocking
I should've rose

from my passive spot along that wall to escape that cold rock and turn true to your soul to reach out my accepted hand and brush your semi-smiling cheek to move free any errant lock that might intervene on the motion of my obvious decree that my body like my heart were ready to love and serve that my passions though wild and hurt were primed to burst and in that moment our body's wants and our heart's sputter would drown out our doubts and you would know if our kiss would've been one that you wanted
but I nodded
heart too thick with doubt
hoping beyond all reason
that you would return my
confession

Yet this is not how a story of limerence begins.
This is the start of my great heart's folly,
a journey on the road to Malthena. Sins
would be the flame that guided my midnite
drive and I, the untested, could only swerve
when the rail was in sight. Still, I tried to stay
on the right side, but that inner demon obeyed
demanded the entirety of my dripping plight.

9

I didn't need a deal with Hypnos to forget the pain as it happened in real blows. It is with some relief that I admit, my memory of crucial details submits to hard bleed. I know you were too kind to solid the deny in my hopesick mind, but all fault for wrongs post that talk weigh on my prolonged redwoods of a world that no longer had the oxygen to grow tall. Having touched your hand and remembered your companionship, I was split deep and withered by your decision to wait a bit.

And in my heart
and with sparking keen

I knew your words
were the kind shove

of a crush
that should only
squish all
between my ribs.

What maturity I owned, I held for maybe the hour until my eyes crumpled shut. And fuzzy days that followed, not even a week. I found no rest from wanting, but accepted my fate as rejected but cherished by the person I loved genuinely. And were my story a fiction writ by pen, I'd have ended it and shown total how a wretch became a man.

But I failed
to be so noble
when memories
kept skin warm
by your hand.

I tried with great conviction
to burn my reserves of hope
and choke upon disappointment
but the tears seared deeper
than calcine refinement.

Having recovered from rape by pushing out reality with a planned coping strategy, I came to learn that what I thought was discipline was my brain waylaying signals long before they finished the full crisp of anguish honest. My loneliness would no longer seep away like alloy impurities, I had to melt with my sin and accept at last a life twisted wrong from deep inside me, but I lacked the safety, wisdom, or wings to fly free.

All I could hold onto
was that tender check of friendship
against my sprawling regret,

or that assurance past midnite
that my heart beat wasn't wasted to surge
for you, or see the true spiritual bond
that connected us beyond words
or action
or failed physical attraction
without the mistake
I couldn't even build
from the hormones
unquenched and lonely

So for the first time in my life

I held my own hand
and squeezed to my chest tight
and dreamed with shame nova bright
that I hugged your body
and lost all sense of suffering
thinking that hand that held mine
was no connect by folly
but a longing your soul did feel
in the way my sobbing chest
found relief by embracing
that festering sharp memory

10

You were crystalized and shattered
with every moon's flight,
and I, the demon's hammer,
thought I was winning love's fight.

Brundled, my skin peeled off with elongated resistance. That monster within, that visceral thought gone human hybrid without reason to persist, looked to be what I felt in honest. For I was a wreck then and always, an abomination of human creativity bonded to pest.

Your rejection accepted in some place deep inside
there was a feral justification that your insight placed me
exactly where I belonged. Not wronged, but sorted,
sent back to my walled cage to eat the scraps of yester
and pick out all that festered.
Turning over rot
grinning with my sallowed teeth.

Beyond hallowed dreams.
I harbored secret flames,
longed for your enlightened apologies:
for all the nights wasted
with us grit and pasted
crushed by a soul unpaired.

Mad for masculine hunt
seething to chase your run
breathing not to calm
but by instinct
as primal devouring
left my honor as carcass,
as we did not what was best
but what hormones craved.

But still then even as I dreamt -and I mean it full in those storm wrought oceans of Baku pools- of stabbing knives to chests, of biting necks, of gripping bodies naked and taking whatever wicked wants my flesh kindled,

I kept you far from my lips
I did not hold up that forbidden kiss
as a thing that would one day occur
nor did I ever picture,
not even in dreams,
of you and I drawn together
by the passion of bodies
made to fulfill programming;
dirty though biological.

What made you
a shade under yew
those poison pains
I unthinking flew,
kept you off brain
your mien unchewed,
cuz I still knew
you were not mine
and were free to fly.

But that flight
from a smirk to star
to a flirt in my mind
drove my crazed chaos
to knuckle tight pathos
and week long pity parties
explaining lonely
by my wicked limbs
and every desire unholy.

But still then, even as I wept -and I dried my eyes on every willing shoulder, forgetting prudence, ignoring subtlety, never once giving the space for you to breathe, and be, and truly think how I weighed when compared to we-

you were a friend complete.
Though guarded as always
you gave me counsel,
heard my wallows,
read my letters,
and wrote back sincere.
I got more than I deserved
but acted entitled
to a day at your side

or the reason why stutter
came from heart's flutter.

And I used that road between us
to grow a garden of deception;
planting seeds that betrayed trust.

11

Without complete rejection,
unable to burn wants to memories
I worked with splintered dedication.
Polishing my visage while ugly
familial patterns sought to learn
your soul's tapestry:
from heartstring
to mind defend.

Born to the blinding stage:
of parents directing cope,
of ratking needling string,
of our world's slow dying,

I was made to perform lines with passion
speaking of what's inside whether tired,
whether conclusion made sense of hurt,
whether or not my soulrot seeped clean.
I worked weekly to help my family
construct their corrupting mythology.

The thread always returned
to the same burn marks
on my skin sack
stitched tight to smother
but too loose to cover.

I was the perennial problem.
My selfish ills.
My pessimistic refusal
to cease my screaming
and accept my life
was better than most.
My mind always calculating
a world where clean
meant no pests devouring.

Freed by your grace,
crying, I repined for

ascension
from roach feed
to human body;
not even dapper
or suave charming,
but simply normal
enough to be wanted.

For this, I was mocked.
Called gay by friends
scorning sensitivity.
But I fought on
to be more than filth
for I thought a better me
could show that I
was indeed trustworthy,

to know the full sky darkening trauma
that was the storm that kept you safe
in that tall nocturnal tower ivory,

to know the shape of your anxiety,
to be a hand you crave and request,
to be the friend and lover you let in
and explain why you were so haunted
and together we'd dispelled thoughts
of liberating suicide.

But for all my efforts
to turn that monster liquid
my mind was past hurt
beyond myopic bitter
real distort' introspect'
it worked in ways
I couldn't notice
let alone prevent.

The spider eggs in my brain
laid young and replenished
with every fight and rant
made a weaver of me
like ophiocordyceps
from arachnid to fly trap
I respun our every interaction
to our love's new mythology.

Reframing our every conversation
into some larger proof of our destiny

trying out different reasons
why my observed reactions
meant that I was right
not just for you
but for any woman
in your same position.

Were you too overwhelmed by life
to notice the way I shifted the past
to conform to the future I ached for,

were you too uncertain to craft
a tale of motivations and acts
that conformed to what actually
was,

I may never have been something decent.
I would've strayed for reason,
accepting that your love
was proof that my soul
was worthy of unfettered bliss
without me doing work
to be more than a wretch.

But you were smart enough to realize
that my version of us
wasn't the same from August
to winter and yonder.
That my mind wasn't merely
cloudy but conspiratorial.

12

Now gone,
now that we
will never see
each other again.
I can admit
to myself that

these myths are nothing more than words. I was your friend and you were so much better than patient. In reliving these injustices, I hope to see how I am, so that I will never repeat the worst that I was. I know that there was no monster within, no mind spiders controlling how I reinterpreted what happened, no childhood pact with Hypnos. But what I am wasn't what you deserved and I have always been grateful that you would not accept me when I was so close to my worst.

Even though I have tried to see past the lies that other whispered into my ear, I faltered. Even still I falter from my self, from seeing the wisdom and even nobility in what few actions I took with a simple desire to respect your will, to honor your decision whatever it might be.

For so many nights,
for so many years,
when I retold my plight,
and explained youth's fear,
smiling supportive faces
said I should've taken your hand
and kissed with ardor;
showing with passion
what our bodies wanted.

Both you and I knew that we could've loved. We knew it without ever pressing lips together or growing naked and trusting the other to express affection from skin to skin. We knew it because romance does not begin with sex, it is but one way for hearts to connect.

Before all of the wrongs I did to you,
before all your best efforts to drag
my mind out of my pit,

we understood each other. We understood who we each were with as much candor as we could possibly express and there was a connection, a path from person to person. It may not have been a road from your evil Goddess to my wretched self destruction, but it was a bond of words built with trust and communication.

That's why I wanted to know that my confession was felt both ways. That's why I waited to hear that you loved me too before ever kissing you. No matter what was going to happen I never would've kissed you until you wanted that from me. I never tried to force anything and you knew that. You knew that until the day that you could no longer trust me and I hate that things had to end without you being able to look me in the eyes.

But I don't hate you
for making that choice.

13

My adoration must've been terrible. In all the scary pull of the undertow that was your depression, you saw only how your spirit was drowning, thinking I loved you for your complexion or your facade, but I was drawn in by a depth of compassion that reached into my heart like my walls were illusions because your weren't ill at ease to pierce my deflections and start a dialogue that took an hour to resolve. It broke my heart to see your defenses remain unchanged by my insistence that your existence was beyond a mere craving, but a saving grace that I needed in spades. I was beyond reason to view your face for that gorgeous mind inside was so far away.

I was lost in that sea of doubt, battling my own depression as I tried to swim out to your hand. I thought less of a kiss than giving spiritual chest compressions, but my perceptions of perfect empathy led me to compliment incessantly – hoping that praise would burn away the malaise and get you to realize that I was capable of materializing a limitless love that would endure your worst. Of course, the curse of my trauma, the lies of my abuser, cast a cruel spell on my well meaning intentions and put a dent in the rusty armor I polished.

Yet, you weren't complacent, nor were you intransigent. Hearing my rants, you lent sympathy even as you stopped my love bombs to express the belief that you were beyond pity. You told me you were wrong, that your darkness was more than a glib song of regret, but a state of being you lived with and that only piqued my interest. I may have trampled over your feelings in my attempt to keen the shape of your misery. It sounds like me.

I think in some way, you may have thought that your wrongs would've scared me distant but my resistance to drop the discussion of the loneliness of your bed came not from thoughts of being good enough to change you, but a fear that I would never be worth enough for you to share true. I conceptualized many tragedies in your past and urges so wrong that a good Christian would bile-hack.

Did you cut? If so, I would've been there to offer resistance.

Did you purge? I would've been there to squeeze as you fought the urge.

Did you suffocate? I would've been there to transfer your hate.

But my ruined state proved to be an unreliable comfort, didn't it? I had this odd sense of morality, a funeral kind of justice that made compromises seem like a hot mess. I know now why my trust was never earned, for that trust that I coveted more than your body was never given the respect you deserved. I acted like a kid on Christmas waving about a wish list. I felt so entitled to share your deepest internal indictments that their denial felt like a total condemnation; my very mind on trial, judged unworthy to share your dirty burden.

But you know this wasn't the worst of my missteps. For your recovery came with my worst moments. I wish I could go back and shake myself into giving healthy takes on lighting that void in your lonely nights, but my fight was with myself and I had not the optics to truly look beyond my hell.

14

Jealousy chewed inconsistently.
At times the mere mention
of you meeting a guy
sent me into frothing.
Others, I hoped his hand
would light that darkness
and warm your coldest regrets.

The first time you talked about being romanced
with some uncertainty about their intention
I was certain they were smitten.
The thought of you meeting him
for coffee or conversation
made me sick to wait unknowing,
but I never even thought to ask
if you would let him inside.
For in asking that, I would have
to admit that I wasn't permitted
to know why you suffered.

Was it your brother?

But another time,
my friend fretted for weeks
trying to chew on thoughts
of you and he sharing laughs.
With fear, he told me
about how he crushed
and I gave whatever
small blessing I could.

Another friend
only mentioned
that he'd been spending
nights at your house
growing close
to you and your fam
and I fumed
ruining a night
of fraternal fun.
I felt replaceable.

But then there were those strangers at college
meeting them alone on grassy hills
while you practiced guitar

and read poets
-I never appreciated
or tried to understand-
those men seemed
fine
then.

Why?
I can't say.
I could never say
what made me
mad or manic,
strange or
psychotic.

Because it was all
about mental health.
I was ill.
I didn't have control.
You tried.

I know better than anyone, how you tried to help me grab hold of my darkest urges. You struggled with me to get me to write down a list of things I like about me and when I couldn't write down a single thing, you burst out with a light that still makes me cry, and wrote down things that made me better than filth, but still I couldn't say any mantras of self confidence. I couldn't find the will to break past the barriers of my deflated interior. I couldn't even convince myself that ego was a necessary part of life.

I had to learn that lesson the hard way.

I suppose you heard about that.

How I isolated myself

rather than admit

that my friends liked me.

But you didn't go down that path of self destruction. You were driven. Smart enough to know you couldn't do this on your own, you didn't stop at self help mantras and talks with friends. You got therapy and took pills to reconstruct your brain's chemistry, and I...

I saw that road between us.
Felt you growing further
as you learned to run
and instead of celebrating
I was consumed

by the parasites
that lived within.

You had the courage to look me in the eyes and tell me that now that you were on anti-depressants, it was easier to show affection towards me, to see me with warmth instead of distress and uncertainty and I accused your feelings of being the result of feel good drugs. Implying that you didn't even know yourself, that you never knew who you were or what you felt or why you felt it because that's who I was. Through my projection I was despicable and horrible.

I will never forgive myself.

I should've been happy.

I should've been delighted

that you had found a way out

of that prison ivory

but I couldn't look past

my own impotence.

15

It's easy to look back at past
bad summarizing reflexive
that I was a pest, a monster,
lust driven hunter. But my acts
were never so direct as that.

My ghoulish eyes did blink
bringing 'bout clarity
reason calm, correcting,
instead of defiling
to build false myths.

I know good moments
must've been attached
back there,
lost then,
in the hazy silt of past.
How I reflect,
how I gaze yester,
is through a slant mirror
warped by tantrums,
broke furniture scratch,
yet still made to distort
with my self immolating plan.

Those good moments
must've been real
for how else did one so wise
show me kindness
and suffer my indignities
and let me lay my hands
upon her to rub aches
to share a shoulder's side
to give friendly comfort
if I was naught
but sinister guile.

Though I can remember nothing good
not a single extended moment
of my presence revitalizing,
she was soft, sweet, and kind to me,
despite my rewritten tragedy.

And were I truly a bitter biter
a jealous slanderous sulk
she never would've tried
to help me pick up my mind
finding wonderful in the hurt.

Because there was something
some small overlooked
bit of redeeming essence
that I could never see then
and I still cannot see now.
Her tear sticking kindness
blinds me to that mirror bent
showing a life out of focus
but undeniably worth her mend.

I know this now
as I should've known it then.
For why else would she try
to be this guiding friend?
Why else did she love me
and say those words
before her trip foreign?

16

I remember your excitement
prepping for college abroad.
A summer of art and wonder,

a time to meet boys with
none who could judge.
And I, as always, was split
wanting you to love
hating that I couldn't give.

But still I tried in earnest
to be the friend you deserved.
I came upon your door.
The hour was predawn early,
I must've woken at four.
Prepared to walk home in ten
you argued for me to ride
along to the port's lanes.

And in that chaos, where cars honked to breathe.
I got out to lift bags, ready to stand forgot,
you closed that distance willing
and pulled me into your hug.
Grateful for a touch so tangled
and I was content for that much,
but with your head beside me
you whispered gentle of your love.

And in your eyes I saw apologies
that what was said we had no time
to discuss. And in broken mind
I was not wanting, only worried
that your words meant a true goodbye.

On that ride back I cried pure ugly,
melting into the child I played.
Around the eyes of your family
they knew not why I was so wrecked.
But for once, for one small grace,
I learned to respect your silent wish.
I did not repeat your words to them
and kept them gloomy in my chest.

For those long weeks I wondered
what it was your love meant.
Had all your best been squandered
before you went to find first romance?
Would you find someone to desire?
Would you give a lover consent?
Would you know the kiss of fire?
Had I wasted my only chance

at happiness? But then my bliss was all second,
it was a thing gone I missed.
As your friend it was my purpose
to listen happy as you told
what you trusted me to hear.
But I could not wait so noble
when you whispered "I love you"
sincerely into my ear.

17

I will never understand why you said those words so true. I will never make sense of what that wretch meant to you. I expected you to come back changed, with a girlfriend or a fling notching your belt, but you were in all ways the same. You were that kind enigmatic beauty who had danced and kissed and still kept everything I longed for close to the chest.

The gift I received, a clover, and a letter writ sincerely. But those words you penned were hollow, more subtle than revealing. I was so wroth to read them when I wanted some deep explaining. And I raged about a pointless gift, some expensive trinket your bought when connection was lacking with that friend.

Upon your brow that disappointment, was apparent and deserved. Seeing your scorn I knew then, I had no right to ask about the quality of your love. I was still too full of jealousy, too immature to be relied upon. So I tried my best to live on without you and committed my heart to a tragedy I produced.

Again, our tale could be over, and I might've lived on to be at your wedding day, but I lacked that crucial skill of temperance, to hold back a pinhole in a dam. With time my heart's pain kept on burning, souring happy days and intimate talks. Though I knew I should stop my waiting, I still wanted our friendship to bloom into love.

Again your form I shattered
and you melted from my lament
coming together like liquid metal
you rose up Godly, strong, driven.

I couldn't stop that damning cycle.
I could never end the limerence.
Though I tried with all sincerity
your warm touch melted my resolve.

As you gained clarity, as your youthful charm aged to womanly splendor, I ached to help your rise to grace by being a stepping stone. I talked up your friendly encounters and asked sincere about your heart's pound. Er, though

I was, to keep our love within, I tried to be an ideal friend.

Hoping to join your delight, wishing I could share your growth, I listened to you play guitar and tried to join as an untrained chorus. I heard your talk of poets and endeavored to assist your struggle in math. You saw more good, I wouldn't hear of it. I only wanted to be crushed so low that I would not dare to hope.

Yet in my jealousy I betrayed my wants. Your dance with art, proved I wanted to be an artist. Hearing your encouragement, feeling I might not be empty within, I followed you down that artistic path and tried my hand at the pen.

And though I wrote like shit
and tried to make drama
from replacing a screen door
you were there to read my words
you were there to encourage
when I thought I a bore.

I wrote poems to try and join you
and stuck to quatrains.
Rhyming every end.
Making you roll your eyes
as slant rhymes
were twisted
into needing accents.

Still even this wasn't enough
to put my beast to bed.
I loathed my failing art
and feared reading Plath
would be your death.

For suicide was always with us.
Our talks frequent spoke oblivion.
We were beyond morbid yearning,
we longed for that sweet liar's end.

18

From the first day I met you I thought you off limits.
You were the sister to my brother's friend.
My kin was my statue's carpenter,
the one who shaped isolating regret.
And your brother was no kind savior.
I knew at once he worshiped death.
Locked into talk of necromancy

your brother and mine looked to Crowley.

We played their games like children picking hats.
What elements we tried to harness,
I think neither longed for sabbath.
Reading the work of Alistair
I realized that cult was built on sex
and having suffered my brother's
attention at the very least, once,
I fretfully kept my distance. Scared.

There you were, this vision of beauty.
Told you hid in a tower ivory,
I though each glance my last.
Knowing now that you wouldn't
attend school, that your anxiety
was a crippling force in your life,
I wonder if the reason wasn't biology
but a costly coexistence beside a bane.

I'll never forget that night we played
at being cardamom sweet and soft
enough to touch so dangerous.
How you let me rub not just feet
but to move hands tender
upon shoulders sore and back
holding the weight of the world.

How you giggled
how you moaned
how I thought
our love could
blossom true.
If only that night
might continue.

Then out came your brother
with those scissors brandished
like a knife, a face with spite,
a wicked dead in his eyes.

His life a sorrow then,
made morose from an online
flame turned to flickering
unread, and open disdain.

What pain he suffered
what goals he pondered

what bloody thoughts
he entertained as we stood
close as us upon that floor,
I think we both know
what ends he thought
to bring to me, but now
I wonder if those plans
included his sweet sister.

19

In that moment, when you shouted his name in horror,
I hadn't seen the scissors. I hadn't know what he held.
I only knew his heart was breaking while mine swelled.
Even before I knew his rage's shape, I became a warrior.
Standing between you, I bore down his wrath and stood
tall as I could. I know he thought me a weak disposable
thing, but I would've fought to bleed. We understood
what malice was in his mind, and so I caved reliable.

Telling him that all was fine.
I talked to ease all in his mind.
I told him at once we were friends
that nothing would ever happen.
And I didn't care what you thought
of me or my cowardice, but it was
something that needed to be said,
to put his rage back to bitter fret.

After that,
things blur.
I think I was
sent home. I
worry how
you had to
administer
your comfort.

Years later, after we had failed as friends, I saw your brother in neutral ground surrounded by former allies. Earlier he had joked about scissors, as if his threat hadn't been a criminal act. As if he didn't owe me thanks and apology, instead of derision for softening his emotional high. I asked him then if you were fine, if you had found happiness at last. He laughed, as so often dark he laughed, and said that he was with your husband's sister, as if that explained all I fret.

I don't know what kind of terror he was.

I don't know what horrors you survived.
I only hope that instance was isolated,
that you lived comfortable as you might.
But I know first hand a brother's mercy
when their minds suffer delusions grand.

Many suffer anxiety
without any cause
or stimulus.
How horrible
it is to hope
that you were
such a case.

20

After saying those of words of distance,
after seeing how close I came
to falling back into that trap
of thinking you and I endgame,
I think I tried in earnest
to really live on without
that thought corrupting me.

For a time I might've even tried to seek out those who would quiver my heart, since you I don't think you ever talked to me about those words of love beyond a dismissive comment about you being wrapped up in the moment. I don't think we ever talked about your brother threatening my life or what that meant about your relationship with him. Did he think he was protecting you, that you couldn't tell me off by yourself?

Moving on was hard, but I did my best. I spoke out against destiny and came to write what would be my first attempt at a novel. I was driven to writing in those pages, in showing how thoughts of love as this reflection of perfect was a curse upon the mind that kept a love that required growth in the realm of fantasy. But I never meant to write him as me or you as she, they were not ever allegory. I only wanted to write a message that might spare someone the pain that I carried.

And in the scary cross of time,
where events bricklaid
now seem junksplaid.
I don't know when my
resolve to move on
wavered that threat.
I can't even order
every event correct.

But I know you inspired my art.
That you gave me goals to strive for.
You saw my eyes grow bright
as I worked on math problems
and encouraged me to try
again after I failed both
my math classes. I did.
I got a degree and tried
my hardest to be happy.
I worked on that novel
for over a decade, but quit,
and then wrote over twenty
and more every year.
I've finally found a way
to enjoy Plath and Bishop.
I found love. I'm better.
I'm better than I was before.

So maybe I couldn't grow into a human without dying as a monster.
I had a trip of my own that gave me time to write and think of us.
Not just the us that was or that ever twinkling happily ever after,
but the relationship we had; whose full weight still crushed ribs.
In a journal made of forest fibers, I wrote down my feelings honest.
I realized that I was protecting myself from you, preserving that wall.
I'd tried to learn that relationships were a hill of beans, but candidly
I remembered that my love for you was the fire that lit up my all.

Without the feelings inside,
the gravity of my desire
pulled carnal thoughts
down to pitiful distractions.

After years of getting closer
I knew not how you felt
or why you returned
any of my calls or saw me.
We were fighting when I left
and you gave me that journal
as a peace offering. How sad.

I took that peace offering and wrote my mind,
convinced myself to go on without a plan
to interact with you as the moment
demanded rather than try and act
in a way that was calculated,
but soon I knew that my love

would never cease. I hardened.
I stood my ground and committed
to loving you not matter what.

21

my last happy mem with you
was so thoroughly sploiled
that I can't recall a thing
aside from how you asked
in some strange honesty
what I thought seduction
would look like, and I

--fool inside and out--
thought to show desire
through eyes brandished
as candid as the aches
and tempest I endured,

not realizing that you might think
my every errant glance
was meant as come on.
I should've spoke
the lamest pick up
line in existence
rather than show

what I honestly believed
the shape our seduction
might've taken
if only we had
lived our life
by bridging the gap
and completing
that road between.

Was that the last time you tried
to test our relationship
or were those words
only uttered because
it was birthday and you
thought to delight me?

But no. I remember
a certain irritation
burrowed in your query.
It was a quest meant

to fail and I blundered
so spectacularly
that my every gaze
became suspect
then, before, and until
that our bitter dissolve.

22

The day I ruined our friendship
was largely uneventful
outside of my final blunder.
Alone. Trusted.
Waiting for your dad
to drive us to pizza.

Sitting at that small table
I mouthed "I love you"
when that feeling hit me,
and your wrath was delayed
until we could share the
silence of his car, but you spake
all that fury of bonded years
shaken by my limerence.

You thought I was trying to trick you
to share the spiders of my mind,
but I never manipulated by intent;
it came from upbringing
oft against any directed will.
Your kill was executed
perfect. Stay guarded.
Let me leave as a friend
and when next we met
you told me our love
was forfeit. Abandoned.

There was nothing I could say to change your mind. I hope I thanked you then, for your friendship for your guidance, for giving me the love to destroy my walls and expose my heart to all the ills of this world. But I said that all too often. Maybe it would've been best if I said nothing, and simply agreed to every term you set.

I played my part, picking up my things like a stranger forbidden even a word of kindness from any of your family. I was treated like a stalker. They acted like I would harass you and try to force myself back into my life, but I didn't and I would never. All I ever wanted was your consented bliss. We exchanged so many letters in those two drawn out years of anguish and I couldn't keep a single one. I wouldn't be surprised if you burned them.

For years after, I would look at the time and see if the numbers were all 1s, as you claimed to see. And like Fievle looking at the moon, I wondered if our eyes shared the same sight, if somehow our souls were bonded beyond your sentence. I wished that I had

behaved different, that I had kissed you
avoided you from our first introduction,
that I'd never strayed from my devotion
making it clear that I wanted us together
no matter what changes quaked through,
that I committed full to our friendship,
that I could see your genuine happiness.

Mostly I wondered if you still thought I deserved life.

23

you were my first

i was your pest

in jest you were a Goddess

i bent low in service

you claimed the crown of evil

i shivered to receive your cruel

Rejection humbled me. I knew then I was damaged
beyond any pep talk or tender bandaging.
Sentenced for behaving like a stalker,
I too oft longed for righteous slaughter.
No reason to hope, I knew you trusted
once and so I sought love unconstructed.

When I noticed beauty, I kept it hallow.
Only did I follow when some connect grew
or as my isolation corrupted all within. New
love had a way of bursting larger than sense,
so to avoid my worst I asked for dates fast.
I didn't wait for lingered yearning to fester,
the horrors of our yester shook my conscience.
Failed crushes churned to dig my heart fallow.

Oft as I heard rumors of your life without,
I only ever wished you the best; never hunting.
Though I hurt to lose your guiding smile,

I contented myself to survive love's drought.
I endured your absence no matter how cutting.
Inspired by you, I cultivated my artistic style.
Tempted to slip back to a voidswallow wretch,
mem of lost companionship kept heart stretched.

Strained, I leaned to strange ends
thinking my full love too wicked.
Sacrificing all I was to benefit them,
my martyrdom betrayed friends
but brought me a new savior
one who loved despite failures.

And in the minutes that passed,
as the clock clicked from 11 to 23,
I stopped seeing your spirit eyes.
With the anguish of our aeon cast,
I hope you forgive this final mythology
to kill the tempt of limerence lies.

DISSECTION

In the process of sharing my work, a strange thing happened: people looked to my poems with curiousity, not just to the content and motivation, but the forms, the flow, the way I danced around rhymes or avoided quatrains. There were those who looked to me for advice or understanding or perhaps simply asked these questions to motivate their own work to go in new directions and so I feel compelled to share that vital insight, to use this book as a resource for burgeoning poets to consider new approaches.

Poetry never come easy. It was something I fought to create and much of that struggle has come from my personal perceptions on what the nature of poetry truly entails. To create these poems, to make this book, I've had to destroy the thought that an ideal poem takes a certain shape. I think that's an importat part of any poet's journey, but there's definitely something that comes before that, something I don't know if anyone can even teach.

I'm speaking about the artistic impetus.

Every poem needs a reason for existing. It doesn't matter if it is an exploration of form, the telling of a story, the exorcising of inner demons, a shout against injustice, lamenting a love lost, or celebrating a life lived. A poet must have a reason for creating and with it should come an artistic vision that speaks to the style, the form, the structure, the manner in which vocabulary, cadence, and syntax are all tackled. These crucial elements of a poem come from what's inside. It is up to the poet to find what they need.

For me, finding my voice meant an exploration of forms, an acceptance of lyrical flow, a harsh introspection, a relentless anger at our world, and a willingness to accept that metaphor can strike to the heart of a concept better than blunt explanation. Not all of these aspects of my writing work in tandem, and nor should they, but I needed a direction to pave the road forward.

At times I ignored my own rules. I detest meta fiction, or in this case poems about poems, but I broke that rule many times and will likely break them again, because sometimes that's the shape my heart needed to express what's inside. I don't think the point of personal rules is to restict the self, but rather to define an artist's norm, to create a baseline that is judged against the whole.

In creating these poems my baseline for novel writing has shifted and making this book has likely shifted my baseline for writing poetry. In my experience, art is never stagnant. It is a living spiritual presence that can lay dormant for a decade or grow so gluttonous it leaves nothing for the host to think with. It is less a guest in one's house, then a symbiote with a complex relationship with its host.

Art is not gentle and it requires respect.

Every artist must find their own way forward and if writing out a set of hard rules helps to guide the shape of all creation, then do so, but know that hard rules are not simply limiters, they are spiked chains around the neck. That choke will come to inhibit and if these rules become axoims the artist who chooses rigidity may loose sight of their reason for making art in the first place.

Speaking on my rules for poetry, they're complicated.

I think that even lines evoke serenity, quatrains in particular are so familiar they can have a kind of invisible quality to their structure, the unheard beat of a drum. By contrast an odd number of lines in a stanza can be stressing or evocative and I use this odd-even balance frequently throughout my work.

Likewise end rhymes can be inivisble, but they are loud in practice. So many readers have become so tired of their use that they can become an annoyance, a distraction from the message that aims to strike the heart deep. As a result many of my poems not only play with where the rhymes land, but imbed the rhyme in the middle of lines; paradoxically adding more rhymes than are necessary. So I do my best to detect connecting assonance from line to line, from word to word, to see how the ear is being lead by the eye.

Form is something that I rarely follow to a letter. A-A-B-B rhyme schemes have their place, and I will drop them into my poems when I think that ease of tension fits an emotional high, but as a rule I rarely let an entire poem be so predictable. Rhythm is best with contrast and variety. Verses vary from the chorus and are frequently connected by a bridge.

That isn't to say that I never follow a form or structure, it's just that I try to stray from the simple. "Chaparral" is a villanelle and I have included it first in this dissection to show how I tried to tackle the notoriously difficult repetitive form. I've also included poems that use a form that I created full cloth. I firmly believe that a poetic form need not be pre-existing to be used, but every form will have some kind of subconscious resonance that needs to be understood.

In writing my poems I do my best to sink into the work, the meaning, while obeying the rules that I have set forth. I reject the idea that true art can only manifest from raw creative outbursts. A finely tuned artist intuits rules, they internalize them so deeply that they can be all but invisible while creating; this is how the chaotic work of Pollack can fit the aestethic beauty of a fibonacci spiral without consciously striving to fit that pattern--because he internalized the splendor of the golden ratio.

This is why technical exercises are so important to an artist. It is why an artist needs over ten thousand hours to achieve success, because there are a myriad of soft skills that are difficult to identify, let alone hone. Those that want to be a poet needs to commit themselves to free writing as well as highly restrictive techinical exercises, because each offer different benefits. I firmly believe that there is not one single path to artistic success, that an artist must pursue all paths, to learn from all aspects of life.

The only sure truth I can postulate about art is that a creative cannot be indolent. Art requires a sacrifice of time and so for those that hope to be a poet, I implore you to take this seriously and push yourself by reading, writing, studying, tweaking, playing, sharing, and producing poems.

It is my humble hope that showing my thought process will offer some small bit of inspiration as to how an artistic mind can be both technical and ephemeral. The artist cannot follow an algorithm nor be unbridled chaos, they must work until they can intuit both. Reject the false myth that the brain is split and find the way to use all that your mind has to offer.

Chaparral DX

This poem is a fairly major exception in my work, as it is a villanelle, a poem with a rigid structure. The first and third line repeat three times, making for an extremely repetitive read.

The 19 line poem comes from origins of song and so I thought it important to add to the repetitive quality, leaning into the inherent quality of the form. By rhyming the first and third line as well as the first line of the stanza, each stanza follows an ABA pattern with the final stanza adding an extra A, which feels expected when each stanza flows back to A.

"Chaparral"

life is arid in the hilly chaparral
every shade a buzzard from up high
where strange and daunting creatures dwell

what's safe or nourishing is hard to tell
a succulent might leave you withered and dry
life is arid in the hilly chaparral

the landscape a canvas of tectonic swells
each range feels close but further if you try
where strange and daunting creatures dwell

soft leaf dreams are easy to quell
knee high bushes block your stride
life is arid in the hilly chaparral

clear and loose paths mark your cell
as unseen beasts laugh at your pride
where strange and daunting creatures dwell

in the haunt of a rain that never fell
across the sky distant waves mark the divide
where strange and daunting creatures dwell
life is arid in the hilly chaparral

"Chaparral"

life is arid in the hilly chaparral
every shade a buzzard from up high
where strange and daunting creatures dwell

what's safe or nourishing is hard to tell
a succulent might leave you withered and dry
life is arid in the hilly chaparral

the landscape a canvas of tectonic swells
each range feels close but further if you try
where strange and daunting creatures dwell

soft leaf dreams are easy to quell
knee high bushes block your stride
life is arid in the hilly chaparral

clear and loose paths mark your cell
as unseen beasts laugh at your pride
where strange and daunting creatures dwell

in the haunt of a rain that never fell
across the sky distant waves mark the divide
where strange and daunting creatures dwell
life is arid in the hilly chaparral

To add to the lyrical flow I did my best to have the stanza ends keep the choppy 1-2-3 of the word chaparral. Line 4 uses repetitive "s" sounds leading up to the chop of "hard to tell." Similarly for line 10, the "ea" sounds end their repeat to slide into " easy to quell".

Knowing that the same trick can't work forever, I varied my approach in the second and fourth stanza, the alt theme stanzas. Line 7 ends on the chopping 1-2-3 before adding the rhyme. Line 13 backs off from the repetitive vowels sounds and Line 16 has the repetitive vowel sound ON the triplet.

With the first and third line of every stanza rhyming, the poems risks falling into that trap of a single assonance sound, something that I think is actually more dangerous to imploy than a rhyming couplet quatrain. Not that I don't use it myself, but here I thought it best to try breaking up to rhythm with an alternate rhyme connection the second line of every stanza. If I wanted to pontificate about my success, I could try to say I was trying to construct the hills and valleys of the chaparral through rhyme scheme, but it was nothing more than a choice of contrast.

While it's important to follow flow, I think it needs to vary from the pattern; dancing around it so that the patterns return is not simply expected but welcome. From the first line I committed to sounds around i and a and tried to keep to those vowel sounds without being redundant.

"Chaparral"

life is arid in the hilly chaparral
every shade a buzzard from up high
where strange and daunting creatures dwell

what's safe or nourishing is hard to tell
a succulent might leave you withered and dry
life is arid in the hilly chaparral

the landscape a canvas of tectonic swells
each range feels close but further if you try
where strange and daunting creatures dwell

soft leaf dreams are easy to quell
knee high bushes block your stride
life is arid in the hilly chaparral

clear and loose paths mark your cell
as unseen beasts laugh at your pride
where strange and daunting creatures dwell

in the haunt of a rain that never fell
across the sky/distant waves mark/the divide
where strange and daunting creatures dwell
life is arid in the hilly chaparral

Bad Weaving DX

Knowing that forms may follow whatever pattern one likes, I tried out a poem that hides the rhymes by calling back to words within the first sentence of the stanza. This generating sentence needed to contain at least four words, or four syllables if I wanted to be especially sparse. This was how I came up with the form for "Bad Weaving" and it posed some interesting challenges.

Working under the theory that a 5 line stanza would create a sense of tension, I tried adding a secondary repeat of 3 lines where the first and third line only required a single call back to the generating stanza. My thinking was that the 5 then 3 lines would create a more balanced 8 lines. Maybe even contrasting so well that it might evoke some of quatrains well worn ease.

"Bad Weaving"
A B C D
weaving art from dreams
insomnia threading string A′
expelling passions depart B′
leaving eyes dry, head numb C′
tired from heart's extremes D′

guilty like a lush wet from a fling
flattery took over, I succumbed
to a muse's playful gleam
E F G H
brushing off yesterday's bad
a walk of shame fit for a King E′
fingers a comb for greasy coif F′
I take my role as one colonnade G′
supporting a structure in my stand H′

natural gazes redden cheeks to blush
scoff at innuendos in a telling way
until all assume my secret shame
H G F E
bad yesterdays off brushing
dreams from art weaving
D C B A

Playing around with this idea, I immediately tried pushing the rule to its limits on the second set, using "brushing" to generate both "King" and "blush". Then from "bad" to both "stand" and "shame". While I think King and blush worked well enough, I feel like "shame" pushed the form past any coherence.

Lastly I made this form repeat the original words in reverse order to create a sense of coming back as well as closure. Rhyming A to E allowed the final stanza to form a rhyming couplet which I thought worked rather well.

"Bad Weaving"

weaving art from dreams
insomnia threading string
expelling passions depart
leaving eyes dry, head numb
tired from heart's extremes

guilty like a lush wet from a fling
flattery took over, I succumbed
to a muse's playful gleam

brushing off yesterday's bad
a walk of shame fit for a King
fingers a comb for greasy coif
I take my role as one colonnade
supporting a structure in my stand

natural gazes redden cheeks to blush
scoff at innuendos in a telling way
until all assume my secret shame

bad yesterdays off brushing
dreams from art weaving

While I think the form did well enough with two iterations, I do think that ending on a pair of rhyming couplets could have a larger impact, but the reading might not survive such a lengthy jumbling.

Readers only ever have so much attention to devote to what's written. While that attention will vary by the reader's familiarity with genre, I think it's important for a writer to keep the work consistent. An ideal reader can be expected to follow a finite number of details per sentence and the writer should keep that in mind while they edit down the final version. That is, a writer shouldn't overwhelm a reader with too much information all at once. While I don't typically count the number of details per sentence or paragraph, I do try to consider how dense the material is becoming.

New forms, a lack of direct language, hidden rhymes, obscure words, visualization, complex emotions, these strike me as the load bearing weight in poetry. They are the concepts that will drain a reader's attention, if I take too much from a reader, they'll lose interest fast. So even though this poem is 5 stanzas at 18 lines, I find the form to be a little too dense. I may be expecting too much from the reader.

Of course, my working theory of form and rhymes is that they work on the unconscious mind more than demanding active connections from the reader, and if that's true, then maybe the question of density is irrelevant. I might bt able to right an epic 23 part poem and have my readers follow along with enthusiasm.

As a whole, I think this form might add a feeling of confusion, dread, the feeling that things are slowly starting to come together, but it's really hard to say without writing 5 to 10 poems in this form. I do think that single word rhymes referencing the middle of a sentence is great at giving a surprise motion, but this may be a little too structured.

No Sanctum DX

Learning my lesson from Bad Weaving, I reduced the complexity. Instead of four rhymes from a single generating line, it is only three and there is no return of any of the emphasized portions. Each stanza stands on its own, being a poem that keeps its form within a stanza. I think that this allows the piece to be more easily interpreted.

"No Sanctum"

So blind with pride, can't even match the wing shape
to the hallowed highs scribbled on soft birthright.
Perceived divine was a sanctum for cloud rats.
Their squeaked delight never seen past Father's hate.

Lifting sharp time only to examine what years obscured.
Myopic fixation to the witworn plan that treasure provides,
that jigsaw past found from resealed shards lost in tragic
woes for a future only obtained through maladies's cure.

Every break from expectation ignites rage to tantrum.
Pushing possibilities off by frustration for scorn's sake.
Seeing halo's lack as reason to start Armageddon's fight,
ignoring how conviction's rubble leaves no sanctum.

Here my natural tendency to play with form was more fogiveable, in particular "examine" and its slant rhyme "tragic" have a nice interplay, especially as it comes after "provides" in the second stanza. I think the additional freedom allowed me to put more of my style into the page, especially since I wasn't limited the sentence length as much as did for "Bad Weaving" but how does the form read?

It's a little hard to say with my language being elusive and throwing in mid-rhymes, but I think the form adds a kind of invisible stab driving the intent under the peom's surface. Whereas "Bad Weaving" felt like it might've started to overstay its welcome, this form feels easier to digest. I wonder if hiding a rhyme-scheme or form takes more of the cognitive load off the reader.

That's an interesting conclusion to come to here as I'm still prioritizing flow over feeling.

One of the difficult parts about poetry is that meaning isn't necessarily stronger by being direct, that metaphor is generally more welcome than it is in writing. I worry that I push this too far with pieces like this where I wrote a poem with the intent to try out a form, but considering how much of my voice is still present, the larger problem might be my tendency to obscure with metaphor rather than any complication inherited from prose or inherent to poetry.

The poem "No Lullabies" continues on with this form from start to finish. I invite the reader to investigate and try to discern what utility, if any, this form might have.

Sweet Teeth DX

It is rarely my intention to reject what's established simply because it is the norm. Testing other possibilities not only opens my work to new avenues of creative expression, it also has the potential to show the value, utility, and effectiveness of well worn paths. Theory should always validate practice. When it doesn't there is a bias within the establishment or a mistake in the theoretical foundation. Unfortunately, it can be all too comon for these institutional failures to never be questioned.

"Sweet Teeth"

how long
must I feed you
past gongs
your midnight rings true
caressing prongs
catch skin and you
won't leave me to hemorrhage myself clean

in the sink
where I drip
all the cadence
I forget

convergence of moon and stars behind her black
wedding of ancient foes cervine and pack
mixing deadlines and wicked attacks
going til twisted joints break with snaps

how will the thrill dry on your gums

Alternating text has a way of generating movement; simple, steady, motion like a walk or the alternating beat of a heart. Here, by starting with an ABAB rhyme, the reader is given a false sense of stability. I use the line length to expose the chaose bubbling underneath, and by line 7 the rhymes are internal; betraying the tumorous nature of the malicious "you".

The rhymes from "leave" to "clean" on line 7 also establish an early line rhyme motif which I like to use to layer rhymes one on top of the other. Line 6 sets up the change in line length and rhymes from "skin" to "sink", which then establishes a new alternating ABAB rhyme going into the third stanza starting at line 12. There "behind" is continuing the "i" rhymes which are teased with their appearance in "wedding", "mixing", and even "wicked".

"Sweet Teeth"

how long A
must I feed you B
past gongs A
your midnight rings true B
caressing prongs A
catch skin and you B
won't leave me to hemorrhage myself clean
in the sink
where I drip
all the cadence
I forget
convergence of moon and stars behind her black A
wedding of ancient foes cervine and pack A
mixing deadlines and wicked attacks A'
going til twisted joints break with snaps A'
how will the thrill dry on your gums

Here I used A and A' to show the shift of vowel sounds from lines 12, & 13 to 14 & 15. Letting this A to I alternating rhythm continue, even in corruption, until line 16 ends the idea with "gums". An unsatisfying conclusion which sets up the return to the introductory phrase; "gums" serving as a slant rhyme with "long".

Alternating rhyme schemes can also be used to show contrasting viewpoints. I play around with three repeating phrases to create the hum of a mind overloaded.

how long
must I feed you
effortless feast can't still taste so sweet
past gongs
your midnight rings true
must cavities be the thing that saves me
caressing prongs
catch skin and you
were I to rot my meat might claim you
all the rough ravage past savage divide
the hunger an ocean you swum to climb
and honest I go best when sails can rise
but lonely I know these tales won't suffice
when my beat sets meter of your meal tonight
oh sweet teeth
won't you leave me to hemorrhage myself clean

Using a near rhyme to connect "gums" with "long" the introductory stanzas return, but now the rhymes of lines 1, 3, & 5 are alternating not just with lines 2, 4, & 6, but something new and wicked. The artifice of reliable is now all but faded, pushed to bursting as the "e" rhymes gain prominence in the poem. Line 19 mirrors line 7 with "feast" and "sweet" only for line 22 to double down with "vities" matching to "ves me".

Line 25 ends this new triplet of verses attempting to connect "prongs", "sweet", and "you". My thinking is that even in momements of pure artistic chaos, there must be a returning to center to keep hope alive. True dispair is never enjoyable. It becomes a bother to experience, even through a fictive lense. So I strive to keep that contrast of order and chaos alive.

how long
must I feed you
effortless feast can't still taste so sweet
past gongs
your midnight rings true
must cavities be the thing that saves me
caressing prongs
catch skin and you
were I to rot my meat might claim you
all the rough ravage past savage divide
the hunger an ocean you swum to climb
and honest I go best when sails can rise
but lonely I know these tales won't suffice
when my beat sets meter of your meal tonight
oh sweet teeth
won't you leave me to hemorrhage myself clean

As line 25 ends this three form alternating rhyme, our penultimate stanza pushes on the "o" sound along with the "e" adding to the "i" and "a" sounds which builds on what came before while hopefully representing the stress of the situation without overloading the reader. Seeding ideas earlier helps to lessen the mental burden.

Finally, as the "i" sounds and "e" sound dominate lines 30 to the end, the motif is established and I end the poem with a return to the first lament that broke the ABAB pattern. Overall I think the growing form is a bit ambitious, but I gave it a shot.

Doom Colored DX

Often my choice of rhymes aren't so formal or purposeful. The bulk of my poetic upbringing comes from song and so rhymes feels natural and welcome. However my need for divergence and an awareness of a general disdain for lyrical expression keeps me from staying on a single vowel sound, but I am definitely drawn towards that.

"Doom Colored"

dread days don't come
they honor you to stay
to take up residence
in the hopes of yesterday

nibbling on what wasn't said
making cushions of frayed fun
entertained by thumbed solace
any day their home will be ours

Here the "ay" sound, technically the diphthong eɪ sound, fills this frequent roll of a repeating rhyme that dominates my mind. From "days" to "stay" I try pushing some idea with an "o" sound but that doesn't really take shape until the second stanza. I use the start of "residence" to echo "yesterday" by not only rhyming the start, but copying the tempo.

Going into the second stanza, I use alternating vowel sounds to break up that pesky diphthong that I want to lean on. My thinking is that more details help to make the star vowel sound become a bother.

on the casket
by Damascus
drove into mom's heart

feel the brackets
in the attic
shuttering from foul arts

in the pipes
on the lawn
over cobble
across dawn
where the first drops
of the alms lost
in a sea screaming far

did you blink light
or was that shadow

always
on your arm

Starting with line 9 I change up the structure of the poem not to facilitate the use of any rhyme, but to obey a change in tempo I felt building. These short-short-long triplets seem to do a good job of showing alternating pace to build mood. Likewise, I keep stanzas 3 and 4 rhyming only with themselves to divorce this shift from what came before.

Moving into the bridge starting at line 15, I use rhymes to keep the ideas connected but do my best not to lean to heavy on any sonic ideas. I want the rhythm to take over, to lead the reader to feel this driving beat. I don't mind letting the words slip into slant rhymes or lose the rhyme at all because I know I can pick up any dangling vowel sounds when the longer stanzas return. I'm trusting my sense of consistency to create something that flows and on the rewrite I'm looking for meaning and comprehension more that trying to return to that raw creative state.

dread not that pinching ring
nor the hissing burn of rain
noon sulfur calls your name
ain't petrichor dull to tame

when the whips of winds can't keep the foul get out
won't the bawling infants ever
get
out

all the scars of promises
need more cocoa butter salves and an honest
hitch in your jaw
do they expect you to pitch from the lawn?

I'm not always so purposeful with choosing my vowels sounds and so when I lean on a particular sound too hard I'll work to contrast that emphasis as much as I can. On line 26 I use a triple "i" sound to introduce the schwa, ə, in "burn" which I use as an alternate for the rest of the stanza. From line 30 to 37 I let other repetitions speak.

These aren't calculations I make as I write, but a kind of audible aesthetic I try to intuit as I let my voice find the shape of its expression. I will stop when I notice an overbearing repetition and try to find an untapped vowel sound or sonic motif to return to but this isn't something that I consider ideal, rather a necessary loss to try and keep a piece interesting.

after Wednesday debts are accrued
have you tires left to zoom
or will you spend time to delay
that inevitable unenviable regrettable fate
where inedible nights bring ache in bed
from children eating guilt instead

while those daylong guests
repurpose clutter into corner offices
and all those tiny sins
give donation for pulpits
so the doom colored robes fit
in the mind stress made vacant

On line 41 I get lost in the flow created by "inevitable" and let it have its time in the spotlight, but I knew I needed a change on the end of line 42. I could've gone back to the diphthong, eɪ, but chose to draw on "left" as it held a weigh on line 39. That decay, that being beaten down by time is important to the poem and so I rhymed it with "bed".

In editing any number of these lines could be changed, but I always try to consider the risk of over tampering. While I do willfully break advice from others, I always consider the wisdom given. Raw expression is capable of reaching hard truths and so I do my best to get out of the way of my visions, within reason.

I am almost never so cavalier with endings. The outro is important, it is what will resonate backwards and recontextualize everything that came before. Often I do not even start a poem, story, or novel unless I know what shape the ending will take. Exploration can be fun, exciting, invigorating, but it is rarely thematically consistent.

I need to know the ending so that my messaging is constantly pointing towards that theme either directly, through symbols, or word choice.

For "Doom Colored" I didn't have any lyrical ideas, but I understood that these recurring rhymes had picked up momentum and gave them a welcome finale, doing my best to stay out of the way as I let these sounds speak to the truth of the poem's anguish.

as those one time visitors ascend
to the highest office of your coffin
you spend your final days at home
writing an ideal proposal
for the downsizing of your life
to mere memories of those
who haven't lost the love inside
but cry not

they aren't far behind

stubborn vine DX

When it comes to my propensity for esoteric language getting in the way of my work, I think by vine series is illustrative. The idea for stubborn, starless, and surviving vines was to create three versions of the same poem. I wrote each with the same intended meaning but varied the approach.

"stubborn vine" was the first of these and came out to be the longest. The feelings of the piece manifested as symbolic imagery, which I followed to its completion.

Stricken by this representation of art and the artistic project, I let this vine's story grow with a cast of characters of a babbling brook, the rocks, birds, and critters all serving a different but connect role as observer, consumer, those nourished, or inspired. In the end, the ultimate enemy of this creative impulse is the self which destroys all that was wonderful about its creation.

In this final version of "stubborn vine" I don't know how much of the story gets through and I worry that my telling created too much weight on each event, belaboring every change by explaining the story in excess. When finished I compared the three version and thought "stubborn vine" did the best job of expressing not only my vision, but the emotions that inspired the poem. Yet when given a choice between the three none that I questioned preferred the first.

"stubborn vine"

Unwelcomed, vine climbs against a creek who won't speak. Sentimental brook babbles to rocks of channels neither had seen. Yet stone and drip both give in to a curiosity and think about that misinformed ivy. Submerged by strange purpose.

Still green. Still okay.
Leaves grow out but under
that rushing water;
moving too slow to bother
chatting with that slithering.

Out
peaks one leaf.
Climbing sheet

tenderly approaches sky that calms and sighs and gives no goodbyes through hateful summers but already the chlorophyll fails. One timid greeting ends in a crinkling twilight. Clouds darken somber to begin an acupuncture of piercing hail.

Still twisting. Still alive.
Warm sun will come again.
Fast water, furious, subsides.
Back to chill fête with smooth
companions and that ivy

breaks free of the surface tension! In that light of refreshing shine, doth nourishes young hopeful vine! The worst burden shed like dew drops on a sweet tongue past morning's rise. It climbs! So brilliant and alive that all of nature gasps and stirs sublime.

Here comes a victory worth the bluebird's time. He soars arcing interested in the lively thrive. One leaf comes out thicker and bold curling to form a line. That raucous bachelor takes a perch and sings to good minds and warm nests. Let the best feather breasted

mother gather twigs and support this vine. All the creatures loud and small, came to gaze as that space was filled up full. Through a life green and wonderful, a community formed around that miracle.

Yet no trumpets sound to celebrate that climb.
Instead gray comes to dominate the sky.
Still that yellow striped warrior survives.
Amongst doubting creek and oriole speak
the eyes all look on curiously
as splitting vines fall ominously
back to waters taking detritus downstream.

Hark, that light again! A brilliant accompaniment, to that stubborn glorious vine, that had already shook the worst and darkest night. For the first time that climb won't follow a beam up high. It's twisting form went inward, wrapping branches inside edges,

a leg takes shape and steps upon the creek.
A human frame wrapped sinuously
to make an arm raised valiantly,
but the body stops short of chest.
The rest did it's best, but were only vines.

Reaching inside,
it comes for the couple. Mother and father guard
their quintuplets. Giving a flight, they scratch,

peck and bite. The injustice and spite!
What once was a home, the human
now comes for their kin.
Taking the nest firm, it yanks life out from it.
Crushing the eggs,
a wind blows with violence.
Every leaf and twig, withers and dies instantly.
The great opposition to life
now falls to pieces in the stream.

Still the creek
and the rocks
they talk.

starless vine DX

Continuing the vine trilogy, which starts with "stubborn vine", I created "starless vine" second as an attempt to more away from my surrealist imagery and focus instead on capturing the emotions I felt and turning the intent outward by breaking one of my rules and simply telling the reader what I want from the world; how I felt about an artist.

While I included some of the imagery present in stubborn, I used that imagery as a metaphor in a way one might in a character's monologue. By keeping the language simple and reducing attention on forms, I wanted the piece to be direct, and maybe even a little preachy, and the end result strikes me as odd.

It isn't that I don't like "starless vine" it's more like I don't really understand its success. There's nothing particularly gripping about the flow, the language is so simplistic that I repeat words constantly, and yet the end result was usually preferred by readers. It's the kind of feedback that sends me into existential dread.

This result is the kind of feedback that really makes me think that my artistic abilities are skewed or flawed in a critical way. Everything was different after this experiment because I was forced to take a step back and try to be more experimental as I needed to accept that I hadn't perfected a voice, only found more questions.

"starless vine"

I see you.

Climbing against the current,
you grow like ivy
and you've earned it.
Don't let them freak you.

They want a feast to go with their show,
ignore them all continue to grow
up to that light.
Your first shimmer of soul
might not survive a night,
it could wither at the first exposure.
Don't let that feeling own you.

Ignore the doubters outside and within,
begin to trust that thrust for life.
Your soul will shine,
let it be bright!
You'll know you've made it
when you rise up against the stream
to take shape independently.
And the praise will come
and it'll come loud
and you'll inspire others
and feel proud
to watch their success
and know their growth
and you'll breathe hope.

And yet I see you

I see you thrashed by every laugh
and curl up and hide your light.
You could stand tall, you could be bold,
but every setback becomes a goal
of nothing or it all. And when you stumble,
you think it's a fall.
And the thing that gave you joy
causes pain and so you destroy
that very thing
that you came to live for
and what was inside
dies.

When you take it all
you don't leave anything
for the fall.
I wished you'd look past night,
to see the brilliant starlight.

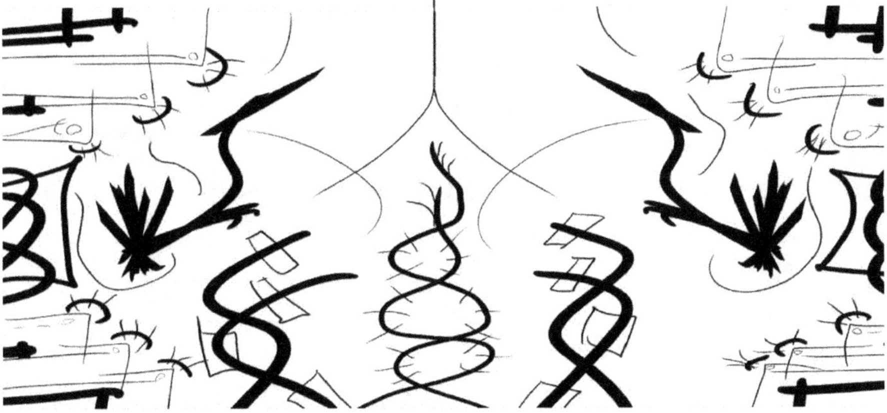

surviving vine DX

"surviving vine" was the last of my vine trilogy which started with "stubborn vine". When writing "surviving vine" I looked back at stubborn and took a critical edge to the work. It's common advice to hack away most of the raw material when editing, but I think that the results show a dramatic difference in impact.

Stanzas are more rigidly defined by keeping sentence length more consistent. Sentences are shorter to get to the heart of the matter quickly. Events aren't belabored, truncating stanzas down to sentences in some cases. One reader described surviving as a better version of stubborn and yet I as a reader disagreed.

I preferred the voicing in stubborn, found the flourishes interesting for their own sake, and didn't mind the time spent in the ephemeral or sensory qualities, and that's part of why this vine trilogy stands out as a sore spot in my mind. My analysis, my impression of these works seems flawed.

"surviving vine"

unwelcomed vine climbs against a creek
brook babbles derisively
yet out from the water
a lone leaf peaks out farther
sun nourishes green tenderly
but that leaf can't leave the drink

it crumbles brown
and goes downstream
a shivering sky
cries hail for thee

past the mourning
sun brings a fresh attempt
in one burst the ivy
rises past surface tension

against all nature
that vertical vine
brings a joyous bluebird
he takes a perch
and sings of new birth
a lady comes to build a nest
supporting ivy with the rest
a hundred critters give their time

yet from up on high
there isn't a faint sign
of support just the pour
of darkness and cruel time

but as Earth spins round
the vine it found

Looking at the piece on its own, I can see what is being attempted, but it feels lacking to me. The symbols come and go with such alacrity that their import is elusive. The flow feels a bit too predictable and direct to create rhythmic interest, but maybe that works in its favor. A simple or direct flow can do a better job of communicating information to a reader and maybe all of my flourishes only confuse when they intend to prop up some better vision of a sonic tapestry.

I wonder if the framing or the scattered cast of characters is really what hurts this version of events or if I'm being a bitter creator too sour that their beauties aren't appreciated. Perhaps by trimming the fat around the details and removing the excessive flourishes, the focus is allowed to be on this fraught relationship with nature.

a reason to thrive
more than the day it survives
the ivy resembles human life
a leg a body with an arm
that stops short of chest
the vines all did their best

reaching for the nest
the birds take the fight
they harry harsh plant
but can't stop the vines
that nest comes out fine
but in a hand of ages
it crushes five young eggs
the wind blows with violence
every leaf dies instantly
that great opposition to life
falls to pieces in the stream

brook babbles derisively

I think what's important is that any aspiring poets sees how this trilogy contorts meaning through a variety of representations. Those emotion, the pathos, the feelings that drive a poem need not be represented in one way or even directly.

Gordita Supreme DX

I'm not a literary scholar, I didn't serve my time in the Dewey decimal's 800 block. My experience with poetry is limited. My understanding of how a form or approach impacts a reader is little more than guess work informed by tenuous connections. As a reader, I've enjoyed deeper dives into a poet's work, but far too often effort to explain a poet's intentions are purely speculative, written by a scholar centuries after their death. It was my hope to try and pull back the curtain a little as my poems aren't always the easiest to digest.

An ideal reader of "Gordita Supreme" is the American Millennial as they've lived through most of what I'm talking about, but time has a way of erasing facts. In as little as one year priorities can shift so dramatically that a limited commercial re-release of a fast food product *should* be forgotten.

"Gordita Supreme"

90s kids will remember,
the prediction of disaster.
The flood of digital fun
would turn us to babies
whining for nutrients,
unable to log off.

They were mocked.

As the digital age was birthed
on a stage of trickle down ego,
honest grifts that popped
a "dot com bubble" before
ambit' homeowners took
"loans they couldn't afford."
From the bitch to the fad,
it was never the street bad
but the wall stayed esteemed
as bits raised home prices
to rates of real estate cream.

From the first line I'm speaking to that millennial culture. As Facebook became a perfunctory part of adulting, "90s kids will remember" became a cheap rallying cry to get easy clicks and milk engagement in the comments section. Yes, I too remember Josta soda, it was a delicious precursor to Monster and Red Bull.

Into line 2, I'm hinting at the fear mongering of Y2K used to make people buy better hardware, but I'm really talking about the rising luddite sentiments of the time. Many liberal arts scholars, science fiction writers, and armchair philosophers warned that an over reliance of technology would melt brains and make people dependent on corporate need.

It did.

I find it telling how in the swell of coming doom people always point to past injustices saying, "they thought that would be the end of the world" when that was an end of the world. The more I have come to learn about Nixon, the more I understand why protests were so needed, why that was such an important time for Americans to keep their rights, but their fighting failed. The yuppies took over, rewrote history, and created a world so devoid of hope that an entire generation stopped trying.

Life changes and as long as those changes are subtle enough, we frogs praise the sauna.

Line 9 is a direct reference to Reaganomics being rebranded by Bush as trickle down economics, an important part of the 2007 disaster that largely robbed most Millennials of having agency in their future. And the stanza hammers home a generation's failure to change our economic destiny by occupying Wallstreet.

Our prize for this eco bomb fest?
Shamed for living off X and babies
as their gen complained of welfare state.
Patriots acting with laughs
as votes regained the right
to be held back by a test,
since racism is dead.
It was killed by cultural segregation,
co-opting a cry for sensitivity
into a mantra of deniability.

Appropriately, the hate lived on.
Growing from buzzy exclusion
to homeland superiority
in the time it takes to read
presidential crime records:
about twenty years
and a bottle of *Stolichnaya.*
Now they'll come to find ya,
online for ancient memes
or outside for alien genes.

Line 20 is indeed talking about ecstasy, but it's also talking about Gen X as "babies" is referring to the Boomer Babies. Line 22 brings up the Patriot Act before going on to talk about the gutting of the Voting Rights Act, a move SCOTUS justified by claiming racism is dead. Moving into the fourth stanza, I bring events up to the 2020s; this poem's present.

Documents connected to foreign collusion in the pivotal election of 2016 were so extensive that they would take about 20 years to read. But much of this stanza is still referring to racism and that hate living on.

The "buzzy exclusion" of line 30 is talking about Buzzfeed and how it made a dot com industry out of cashing in White guilt. Trump's election played a key role in 90s dreams of equality being decimated, but many Millennials are afraid to speak up because of "ancient memes" specifically the racist ones where people got a kick out of breaking taboos. Cancel culture ruined many lives in real time and many Millennials that hopped on that bandwagon had similar skeletons in their very own closets. So they know firsthand what they risk by speaking up.

Going back to line 26, I claim racism was killed by cultural segregation and this is a point I come back to in other poems with the Defiant section.

Melting pot was more than just a theory or observation in the 90s, it was something to celebrate. The intermingling of cultures was seen as ideal; a way to bridge gaps. This was dismantled by claims of cultural appropriation thrown at anyone wearing a rastacap, to the point that enjoying chilaquiles meant trying to earn clout; as if we were all still living in the table dancing number "La Vie Bohem" in Rent.

This is part of why I don't want to rally the populous. Many who seek to create ideal ends instead create the conditions for opportunists to weaponize kindness. Cultural engineering is not as easy as idealists believe it to be. Actions demanding social change require more thorough analysis to be properly implemented.

But the 90s are back!
Don't have a cow,
put that stick
in your bunga!

Bell and Taco's Excellent Ad Venture
revives the Gordita Supreme,
eyeliner, goth 'tude, and black shirts
from a band enthusiast's wet dream.
Who minds if the scene
is dom'd by the same Princess?
Kids like Nirvana,
we can resurrect slut shaming!
Re-up the corp grifting.
Pepsi's got Harvey Danger
raging against the machine with 'zines!
The revolution starts with a cravings box!

With the historical context surrounding Millennial ennui at last established, we finally get to the Taco Bell of it all: a perfect symbol of corporate cultural appropriation if ever there was one.

Here I go into full shill mode to hype up the reintroduction of the Gordita Supreme. Lines 40 drops a Bart Simpson quote and line 42 links that with TMNT Michelangelo's catchphrase "cowabunga", which was used by Bart Simpson for a brief time. Line 43 is a reference to Bill and Ted's Excellent Adventure. "Flagpole Sitta" by Harvey Danger was used in the Taco Bell commercial.

Lines 49 and 50 have the unfortunate side effect of implying that I think Nirvana somehow promotes slut shaming. It doesn't. I don't think. Don't at me.

The reason I bring up Nirvana isn't because of their lyrics, or allegations against any member of the band, it's because of Courtney Love. After the lead singer of Nirvana, Kurt Cobain, took his life, many unfairly maligned his wife, Courtney Love. Some even went so far as to imply that Courtney murdered him and it was a common talking point that she only ever slept with him to help her band blow up.

They had a daughter.

The treatment of Courtney Love was disgusting, but it's very much in line with the rampant slut shaming going about in the 90s. This was the age when a national trial took place to talk about the President's infidelity. By contrast Trump abused his power to cover up sexual assault and SCOTUS said he's above the law. The idea that a President would vacate the office died with Nixon.

Going back to the poem, line 48 is talking about Taylor Swift, a figure who became far more relevant to the 2024 election than I thought she would. That princess was dominating the music charts as she had been for years. She's also a blonde in the spotlight and America has a history of attacking famous blonde women that predates Courtney Love by decades, but she was the obligatory target of the 90s. My comment in the poem wasn't meant to have us call for the destruction of Swift, but rather that she could be dethroned in that same callous way that we dispose of all celebrities.

While the kids who walk our walk
are trained by lower class drains
soaking up donation. A full tenth
of their grind is reading simp lines
alongside their bits and sub times
cuz their hot takes are fast breaks
from the cultivates shakes
of academic excellence screaming
from their own grave,
but kids get that strong dope hit
for every mention of their name.
As legislation comes for loot
but cravings don't stop in that box.

Line 55 is meant to be glib. I don't actually think the modern generation are intuiting the values of the 90s.

Much of this final stanza is talking about streamers, one of the only ways that Millenials were able to find success. I'm deliberately pointing to this predatory relationship between streamers and children because it is completely against the ideals that people were fighting for in the 90s. Streaming destroys anonymity, it turns people into products, the content is frequently little more than advertising the pleasures of a product, and gambling is everywhere. Many big name streamers are paid to play slot machines to an audience of children. So in line 66 & 67 I'm not just talking about loot boxes, but gambling as whole, and how the dope cycle is built into streaming as a product.

Without Scabs DX

Here I strived to craft a poem representing the skewed reality of living in abuse. Details are explained in the most literal sense, but their telling is strained, literally backwards as if see the events in reverse. Interpretations create this narrative of harm passed, of life returning to some state of rest, but there is no escaping the subject at fault. The subject is always at fault because of father's guidance, he'll make sure that this is how the subject understands what happened. Every instigation, every escalation was a result of the subject's fault.

Reality must be pieced together from events half remembered and maybe misinterpreted. Only the clarity of insults, injuries, or material destruction can be trusted.

"without scabs"

up rolls the blood back to the hurt
crimson rain there again domed with tension
sinking into crevices a fissure once shook

shatter clicks and clatters from wall to cup
twirling ever tight to center finding focus
a liquid clear as insults spinning tilted half full

goblin in a hobbling dip cheers to raise an arm
that snarling grin comes to an end
as the cup recovered by gentle palm

that red and green monster settles into motion
creaking down like timber sawed his knees
crashing like a sheet snapped tight on the breeze
what was horrible is now more of a guest
than a pest that can't be suffered to live

and the blood was never there
it was a fantasy
why would anyone care
about the ramblings
of some bag of strings

tied so tight
that none can tell
where its mouth and its tail
are separate

so just forget
about the cup
cause the glass
was never empty

it was always
going to be the last
reason for suffering

and the ring is nothing
more than a marker upon that saucer
like the threshold of a door
once closed aught be ignored
so don't start thinking
that men are evil
when that fine guest
was nothing short of the sort
of friend that people need

none aught to turn away good company
sitting in corners brings monotony
to revelatory praise of indolence

that man rises up from that seat and that cup
that wasn't filled but never empty on that surface
that should be scrubbed clean before he got here

and foot falls sound his exit or maybe follow his entrance
a rap of knuckle to sliced tree brings eyes to a pouring stream
cold pitcher of his water filled wrong for gentle father

Lacking Balance DX

I go back and forth between being proud of "Lacking Balance" and despising it and I've come to accept that it's because of the revealing nature of the content. I don't like talking about my abuse, not the weakness it defined in me, nor the anger it drags out of me, nor the uncertainty that comes from a childhood denying it.

I look at this first defining chunk of metaphors defining my childhood of uncertainty and I hate how rigid the structure is. I'm so fixated on form, on trying to do all these clever things with stanza length and rhyme schemes and I detest the cultivated nature of it, hating that I can't trust my voice to resonate without gimmick.

"Lacking Balance"

back and forth walking on a seesaw
bending knees reacting to outside guidance
blind to the extremes but feeling likely to fall
barely hoping this won't end in violence

mocked for my lack of human defining experience
sexually charged images taunt my ego to small
pieces he mocks for being unable to come together

not caring that holes in my memory defend his innocence
he wheedles my flaws and treats me soft as a feather
for what's strong cannot be cultivated by mere indiscretions

he ridicules my bold refusal to act beyond adolescence
by treating me younger while claiming to respect concessions
but the clear choice to glory is always through horny salivating

shamed into compliance I grow bent in horror's absence
without tearful revelations my mind is pushed to graduating
thoughts of exploitation and lust though I want it none

and my outrage burns unfanned melting my face cereous
every flagellating remark expressing out towards fun
recognizing babies as dumb and every smile the sign of a liar

I grow up witch wicked and my thoughts stay ever serious
my socializing the sum of what is deemed worthy by my sire
thus with no one to conspire with I remain his loyal thrall

yet his castle is more mud than wall
the books he uses as bricks though supercilious
are all unread to add to this delirious notion
that his knowledge is an ocean I'm too weak to sprawl

but my arms work constant
and my curiosity is genuine
and my genuflecting didn't steal
my zeal for a life made clear

of the structure he did violate
so that I might never consolidate
my thoughts to realize this false God
was no more man that maggot

and I wouldn't stand up
when I was a curious beast
made to entertain in a circus
he did conceive

but love wakes me from that dream
and though my paranoia muddles
what should be living Nirvana
I breathe in deep and ignite my rage
and burn all the wax of my face
to walk away burnt but smiling
cause no liar will determine my fate
while the puddles of my tears
reveal the shame of years

spent spinning in a web of silence
but my mouth is all teeth
burnt raw I'm ready to bleed
brutal I'll willingly end this in violence

so let him try me

And I try to have some measure of sympathy for myself, to rationalize the use of forms. Some of the most powerful works I've ever heard have been nothing more than simple rhyming couplets, but that only reminds me that I was too pretentious to even trust that simplicity. I always have to rework the wheel, somehow, in some way, I rework those efficient spokes as if by modifying them I can somehow own their success.

It's a losing battle, this war with myself, because I always find a way to make it all about how I'm wrong.

Talking about this in "Lacking Balance" is difficult. I do what I can to show the way knowledge was part of my abuse, to prove that I have somehow risen above it, but when I know how broken I am all of this feels like a lie.

These feelings are inescapable, part of the ruinous legacy that is my abuse, that makes me live without balance. I shift from one extreme to the other pivoted by a system I did not construct but can't dismantle. For 6 stanzas I speak on my abuse so removed that the meaning might not be clear.

Stanzas 4 and 5 talks about how I continued to have porn shoved in my face, how I was bullied into wanting flesh so that he might use that lust to bring me back to his sexual abuse and I don't know if any of it reads. I don't know if my sorrow scans and that's about as much value as I can put on my brain.

Maybe it would've been more helpful to explain how I can write about what's so painful, but I just dredge up the feelings, cry, and try to get it all out while following whatever structure my mind has grabbed onto.

A Child's Fairytale DX

All innuendos in "A Child's Fairtytale" are not only intentional but entirely the point. This poem tries to keep up this veneer of an idealistic romance while using sexual desire as the motivation. It is how romance appeared to me so often and how men are frequently defined in these roles regardless of the gender of the storyteller or the target reader.

The fact that this poem is called "A Child's Fairytale" is meant to be upsetting. Sex and children should not be thought of together and yet this is so often the suggestion given to children. As this poem talks about the expectations put on men, for me its about what is taught to boys. How we are but animals needing relief to be tamed.

"A Child's Fairytale"

Once upon a lie
her gloved hand in mine
a tandem turn as we glide
composed and keeping time

I lay down steps like a rhyme
making me worthy to find
her crimson lips spreading wide
to tell me I'm welcome inside

her heart's chamber divine
so that I might savor sublime
that carnal hunger that thrives
despite all temperance outside

Secondhand Damnation DX

"Secondhand Damnation" strived to discuss the anguish of craving cigarettes while never choosing to smoke. From line 1 I endeavor to evoke images of smoking stains on a stucco ceiling, but I've come to realize that stucco ceilings aren't all that common. Still the flow is driving and line 2 solidifies this point, but I still feel like this poem about a lifelong craving for secondhand smoke fails to deliver.

I do wonder how often the idiosyncrasies of my writing get in the way of comprehension. Writing poetry, I tend to let my oddness come out unfiltered. This phrase on line 3, "inwards curls fingers" is strained, the kind of thing writers and poets use but a person never would. More natural is "fingers curl inward". But I like how my phrasing shifts the focus to the action.

Line 8 might even be a worse version of this. "septimal gems eye prayers" is a really round about way of talking about the seven gem like eyes of seraphim gazing upon those in prayer. I actually like finding words and phrases that jumble syntax around in a puzzle. There's something beautiful about that to me, like the way "Nude Descending a Staircase" is a collage of geometrical shapes, but is also exactly what the title implies.

"Secondhand Damnation"

gripping tar slipping shards a blade below the stucco
breathing parts boiled dark from a brew tobacco
inward curls fingers seasoned sticky with smoke
raucous shore line deepened by grasping my throat

heaven knows that angels aren't composed of gray
but the fade of want endless drifts by hurricane
wings silent hovering on splintered homestead
septimal gems eye prayers answered with death
each pair a promise to those of faith unbent
the last a beacon leading fog-lost to debt-worn graves
my feet hover as firm hands purple my malaise

I have this fixation with angels being inhuman, it's part of the reasons I bring up seraphims so much. Their seven eyes are frequently ignored, their seven wings serve no natural purpose for locomotion. I'd bring up ophanim, but the seraphim is meant to be the highest choir of angel, it is the choir lucifer came from. So for line 8, the angel doesn't even have eyes, but gems that eye. It strains the mind to understand what's being communicated, especially when this is read aloud fast.

I wonder if the inclusion of angels as a metaphorical tool further shifts the role of tobacco in the angst. My use of angels was to evoke thoughts of death, purity, hypocrisy, salvation, but like angels showing up in urban fantasy, they tend to take up all the attention.

round
round
we lilt level with ground

tilted
jilted
my ange' soothe mewling sound

somber
gentle
my soul flitters half down

whilst
wing
beats
off vital pulses around

and
about
my neck

for that
tar
cloys
my sense

Here the angel also serves as a source of temptation. I am held aloft by the angel, the seraph is a symbol of the temptation to give in to hedonism, to follow physical relief that might fix my defects. The angel is my herald and I use that metaphor as a way to talk about that strange high that comes with smoke entering the blood. But the salvation is that same lie that always accompanies religion. There is no relief, only tricks we play on our brain; regardless of strength.

a child that wants horrors I had noticed
but never worried that shades hungered
after lungs were chewed to shreds
that passing moment of strangers enjoying
the third half broken dark and chewing
long and joyous and stretched to touch my scent

let that seraphim douse
every whim in a bath
I can't remember
her lies came with my cries of salvation
bought in shame's anger
so let heaven's resuscitation
come on lips wide and patient
and through a ghost's kiss
give that gift of life smothering gray hurt

I spent a great deal of time avoiding a direct expression of breath and scent. In the first stanza I tried using shore lines to try and refer to that cyclical motion in and out. The second stanza has "drifts by hurricane", the fourth "mewling sound", and here at last in the penultimate stanza I write of lungs chewed to shreds.

I think there's a great value in subtlety, to allowing a reader to fill in the blanks, but there's always that risk of effort being wasted. Looking at the piece in depth, I wonder if a lack of comprehension comes not in the delivery, but the metaphor. My cries of salvation come with a kind of abstraction, an expectation that a reader is already in the know. It's ironic to think that may have I under wrote.

Mask Slip DX

This poem is about my fears about undiagnosed autism (ASD). My thoughts on this are complicated and I don't think it's worth the time to go into it here. But those with ASD are said to block their urges and I thought that I was pushing back at least 80%. I'd heard about people abandoning the mask entirely and I thought that absurd, dangerous, unreasonable selfish. I dropped what I considered 10% and became a total pain to the people around me.

This line about "praying to obsession" might come off as strange given that I'm talking about ASD, but writing is my cope. It is a compulsory behavior that threatens to isolate as much as my unwanted "expressing wrongs and nags".

"Mask Slip"

I let the mask slip
not fall just tilt
since ideologs saw
a world beyond restrict
asked I was blocking 80

so to save the hypo' press
I let loose a fraction
not thoughts but behaviors
expressing wrongs and nags
that couldn't be 'nored more

I dropped a score of 'haps ten
but the change in a storm
made some run for shelter
lightning teeth and thunder fits
the edge of my noxious within

so the mask's back and I pray to obsession
let the ideos talk as I reform to convention
this little crack may take time to reseal
I won't keen so you'll know it's nothing real

Unwinnable DX

For these last few poems, I kept an early draft and thought it would be informative to show how much the poems changed through the revision process. For the most part the change boils down to length, as a novelist I tend to overwrite.

"proto unwinnable"

we treat mental health like a game we have to lose
there is no winning strategy no grand masters to study
only the suffering and the defeat and the groaning before
we lament our shared fate as contestants relegated
to the sidelines of our own lives but what if we refuse

in truth there is more than art sharing that dying hark
many crippled crawled tall when they couldn't stand
there is a wealth of tales written by those who prospered
and even those who proctor tests meant to segment
those who lick apples from those who bite red sparks

why can't we pull back and breathe embers to flames
why must we smother every promise of calm reprieve
are we not a congress of likeminded biology
is it so easy to believe that crocodiles shake out tears
when all of us long to have a friend recognize pain

not every lament is a desperate ploy for sympathy
sometimes it's an honest attempt to counteract that
ever-present apathy or an unsure hurl of isolated viat
manifested as a message floating on strained devotion
or a preemptive supplication defusing boiling fury

let us face that punishing hate and push til it gives way
to a truth that lends voice to every frustrated heart
for we are the architects of the future we seek
those blueprints are hard but need not be drafted
in their entirety those before implore us to drink

to good fortune and play chords made of notes

from a worldly picked chorus cause experience lives
in the creation of ten thousand years we need not
pick up our ears but learn from a humbling sum
of others that longed to be heard and not forgotten

"unwinnable"

in the mental health game we fold every hand
bemoaning our shared fate from the sidelines
of our own lives but what if we rob the house

there is more than art sharing a long sob
those beaten crippled crawled tall
diligent minds identified winning cards

we need not smother calm reprieves
we are a congress of likeminded biology
we all long for friends to recognize pain

our laments combat the prevalent apathy
they are messages floating on strained devotion
and preemptive supplication to defuse fury

face that punishing hate until it gives way
to a truth that lends voice to frustrated hearts
the blueprints of bliss need not be drafted fresh

we have a world's chorus to join when we sing
ten thousand years of teachers who persevered
a humble sum who longed to not be forgotten

Last Chip DX

I struggled a lot with "Last Chip". It sat in my clump of poems to publish for well over a month. Before I started it, I thought writing about eating disorders were silly, even self indulgent, but people responded well to "Decimal" and so I was inspired to try to be more direct about my experience with binging. In the end I'm proud of the poem and I can even recite the poem under 3 minutes if I go fast enough.

"proto Last Chip"

would that I could reach into that bag
and pull out the last chip gluttony demands
but those crisps by the lip stop my search
they are full and complete an artistic design
each one a bubbled structure ever preferred
to my globular mass more than hollow inside
so my lips smack a kiss and suck all I can nip
and even healthy bodies would forgive one slip

without shame I can chew and enjoy salty fat
no one blames a single taste or even a handful
I mind my decisions but it's temperance I lack
one bite is never savored but requires a coating
my every grasp means to fill my mouth entirely
but even alone I'm embarrassed to indulge

to feel the shove of matter against the back
of a throat that's always wanting overloading
overwhelming me to grab so much I add to the dust
but that feeling is satiated I am always edged closer
being this fat loser who must stop consuming
and so I wipe my hands, stand up, and roll up the bag
but my time away never once had a chance to last

a lick of my corner and my yearning is swelling
that bag of crunchy edges will soon lose flavor
oxygen is a rotting thing no clip can despell
even in the fridge it'll pick up some smell
I've already failed at being a sublime human
my need to feed might subside if I take one more bite

it's only one just for that longing fun that makes me wrong
with a single last chip I can at last be done
but the shape is bent and cracked and covered in dust
the promise of a bag wasted I've only just tasted

so I wipe myself clean and realize with some shame
that the bag is now lopsided and I alone can make
it easier to contain in some corner of my pantry

so that's the only reason I need to eat large fists
it's the symmetry of it that innate order we all crave
is it not human to set things to right and now it's rolled tight
getting up I realize with freight that the bag is now sad
it's a curled up disgrace a sign of my shame
that in one instinct driven moment I emptied it
I alone nearly finished the entire bag in a single sitting
so there's only way to hide the proof of my sin
I must eat it all and even if the edges are sharp
even if the dust makes me cough
even if the oil is cloying
even as the sharpened edges cut my gums
I must eat it all to remove the proof of my fault

but the empty bag means nothing in the trash
my failure to be measured is a night I'll know again
cause every time I'm in the store I think of that taste
I forget how greed makes me stuff my face
how shame keeps satisfaction away
how that lingering peak is always out of reach
how I justify my every devouring
until my feast turns bleak and gives direct suffering

and the bottom of every bag is so gross
I never wanna touch another
but I forget my failure
I long for that perfect chip
if only one could fill my whole mouth
and push all my wants down

but I always pick up another bag
because the thought of being wanting
is worse than hunger reminding me
of the hunger that once consumed
my thought while I sat confused and lost

in school and on my feet
drinking water to stave need
so that I might return sweating
and starving and demolish
whatever product was left for a child
who was never shown how to savor
and only learned how to eat faster

than the nearest rivals regardless
of the chromosomes we shared

if only every chip was as dusty
and oily and small and slicing
as the last I shove into my mouth
then I'd only have the other snacks
to kill my sleep and obliterate
my self esteem

"Last Chip"

would that I could reach into that bag
pull out the last chip gluttony demands
those crisps by the lip stop my search
they are a complete artistic design
each a bubbled structure ever preferred
to my globular mass rotten inside

without shame I can chew
and enjoy salty fat no one blames
a single taste or even a handful
I mind decisions but temperance I lack
my every grasp means to fill
my mouth entirely but even alone
I'm embarrassed to indulge

to feel the shove of matter against the back
overwhelming me to grab so much I add to the dust
that feeling is satiated I am always edged closer
so I wipe my hands, stand, and roll the bag
my time away never given chance to last

that bag of crunchy edges will soon lose flavor
oxygen is a rotting thing no clip can dispel
even in the fridge it'll pick up some smell
I've already failed at being a sublime human
my need to feed might subside if I take one more bite

with a single last chip
I can at last be done but the shape is bent
and covered in dust the promise of a bag
wasted I've only just tasted
so I wipe myself clean
and realize with some shame
the bag is lopsided and I alone can shape

by reaching in deep to eat large fists
completing innate order we all crave

is it not human to set all things right
getting up I roll that temptation tight
just before I reach the pantry I realize
this bag of shame shows my disgrace
revealing my instinct driven moment
I alone nearly finished the entire bag
there's only way to hide the evidence
even if the dust makes me cough
even if the oil is cloying
even as the sharp edges cut my gums
I must eat it all to remove the proof of my fault

but the empty bag means nothing in the trash
when I'm in the store I think of that taste
I forget how greed makes me stuff my face
how shame keeps satisfaction away
how that lingering peak is out of reach
how I justify my every full devouring
until my feast turns bleak and gives direct suffering

and the bottom is so gross
but I forget my failure
I long for that perfect chip
if only one could fill my whole mouth
and push all my wants down

but I always pick up another bag
because the thought of being wanting
is worse than hunger reminding me
of the hunger that once consumed
my thoughts while I sat confused and lost

in school and on my feet
drinking water to stave need
so that I might return starving
demolishing every gift
to a child who ate in a race
beating rivals regardless
of the chromosomes we shared

if only every chip was as dusty
and oily and small and slicing
as the last I shove into my mouth
then I'd only have the other snacks
to kill my sleep and obliterate
my self esteem

U t7t d P4art DX

This is a poem I definitely thought about axing, but I think that experimentation is an important part of growth and so I ended up including my little homage to E. E. Cummings because I knew I would be including these deeper explorations into my work. In tackling "U t7t d P4art" I first wrote out some thoughts I was picking at before transcribing it into the nonsense that followed. I think as an exercise it can be interesting to discern the meaning, but there is a thought bleed that comes when we forgo syntax and experience text as it is.

"proto U t7t d P4art"
albeit in some
ways I know
that my every
protestation is nothing
more
than the
faffing about
of a loser
who is made
no cooler
by the ever
connected experiments
of ballista thrown
fast by unseen trebuchets made decade upon centuries
past throwing
stones far into the future to
destroy not castles but homes
which will soon be the wandering
automachines
that we bleed
the desert lives
to fit all our contraptions in and as long
as we're on the

subject can someone please
object to the idea
that our lived area
need be a plot of land that can be
purchased
when our service to this country ought to
demand something more than debt
and shell shock yet so many
veterans receive the quality of
paperboxes left to rot in corners
that sag from the weight of
unprocessed requests
because the staff is understaffed intentionally so
that these decorated heroes can all decay
to zero
with no chance of recovery because we've built a
society to punish anything
that requires money while still spending
the bulk of our funding
on the war machine
that consumes all genius
while giving back
no stimulus to the same lives that need it

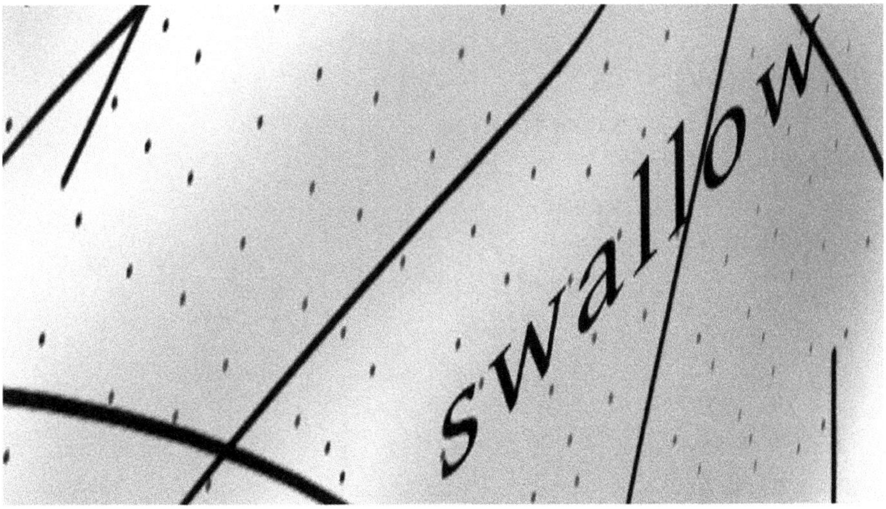

"U t7t d P4art"

a)beit in sm
ways I kn
zt my Ery
prot(station s not)ng
m+
zan ze
faffng abt
f a looooo0000000zer
who s made
np coolR
by ze ver con(nected exp)eriment...s
f ballista thrown
fast by
<{[(unseen trebuchets)]}> made 10ade ^on |c|uries
past thro
wing sto
)nes far in2 ze future 2
destroy ~castles bt homes
which will soon b ze wandRng
automachines
that we (bleed
desert livs
2 fit -V- our contra)
ptions in n as L o n g
as we're on ze
subject cn sm1 pls
object 2 ze idea
zat o(U)r lived area^2
need b a plot
of land
zat
cn
b
purch(a$$$$)d

when o(U)r $Rvice 2 zis country ought 2
demand smzng more zan debt
n
shell shock
yet sooooooooooooOOOOOOOOOOOo m+y
vetRans
receive the
quality f
paper[_]s left 2 rot in
c o r n e r s
zat sag from the w_e_i_ght f
unprocessed requests
bc ze $taff s _R$taffed inten?onally s,o
zat zese de*cora*ted heroe$ cn -V- decay
2 zero
w ~chance f R+ry bc we've built a so-s00-society
2 punish
anyzng
zat req $ while still $pending
ze bulk of o(U)r $undng
on ze war machine
zat consumes -V- genius
wh!e
givng back
~$timulu$ 2 the sm livs zat need .

Untitled Part 113 DX

When drafting this final poem hours before the end of 2024, I decided to leave something raw to be considered without the artifice of polish and reshaping. I left the title as is, an autogenerated clump without meaning so that a reader might interpret what they would from the work without influence.

I also thought it would be fun to edit this poem a few different ways as an exercise, renaming each poem as I went. While I could do this several times, I have a deadline, and I don't know how long it's going to remain interesting to me.

"Untitled Part 113"

I only remember accomplishments
so that I can lament what I've lost.
My gains all came with a steep cost.
My brain reconvenes all my faults
to discuss the bold third option.

I won't be defined by the drip. I can't let my convictions slip. Not for the tears. Not for my legacy, but to scoop up the wreck wrought by my smiling family. I can't let the mistakes of their sage advice take center stage in my life. I can't be the forgotten dream of a self appointed visionary who needed to rape to feel inside.

A victim's right is to keep spitting alive. I may be splitting internal but my bones are still rigid. Defined not by my trauma or the bed that they made, I have to stand tall, to step deep into the tide. If I can grit teeth and try to make waves instead of calling out a false cannonball, I will be an object worth seeing. I won't falter. I will make a splash that leaves suits ruined by bromine and monocles in their flutes.

Their ghost is gone. I'm the one haunting. I'm the one who walks the dark, my wail this nightly typing. Cause it ain't a pipe dream that I've got the drive to slice lean. Chopping that fat as

I attack every last act to the satisfact' of the fat cats and the ghouls beyond me. I want the mausoleum. I want a stone bond that'll reach up and give a reason to keep living.

I want to be a song in the hearts of the dogs of this prison. I envision a world where my dropped lyrics are told from every light box they hold. To be a stellar reprieve from stories that launch brand new, old, but this narrative I gleam is a worm on a demon's string.

I chomp long, chewing on as I take my next bite. Swallow down the tallow, along with Mephistopheles's grin. That silver line within scraping my deep barrel. The tar I seal my cracks, coming off to let in the terrible. And I could laugh wicked as drops of praise make me vulnerable, to a single kick hitting like a brick as a swing on my own gallow.

My books are nothing more than compiled data files. No critic gives me a second look. I bore bibliophiles. I got no style. My substance a gross mess of thoughts juvenile. It's time to grow up. I gotta shut up and take kicks like a can on the gray mile. The pencils I push need to rub the tush of a pig slurping a nation's throw up.

The grind is clear.
Close eyes to fear.
Bleed long for dear.
My swan song ain't near.

I'm not collapsed. Get collected. Send out apps. Work my station. Be a cog. Do the job. Find a way to flee the nation. I can pick apart where they went wrong from another coast. It's better to live and suffer injustice than to be a venerable ghost.

I got a long list of grievances and twenty-five books behind me. Let the words of art die. Achieve life. Reject Plan B. The words of freedom are co-opted, they prop up a tyrant. Make a million in Amazon, and add weight to the crusher. Small press gives them money regardless. The monopoly takes their fee no matter what bodies I carve through.

I said I was a butcher, but they're packaging soylent green. I'm right there eating and "God, that's good!" At least I got meat for their pies. This heresy of artistry is making cash with blind views. They drool for cheap crap cause it churns ads the whole way through. And the best my blade can sever is the devil's line that I chew.

"Swan Song"

I only remember accomplishments
so that I can lament what I've lost.
My gains all came with a steep cost.
My brain reconvenes all my faults
to discuss the bold third option.

I won't be defined
by the drip. I can't
let my convictions
slip. Not for the tears.
Not for my legacy,
but to scoop up
the wreck wrought
by my smiling family.
I can't let the mistakes
of their sage advice take
center stage in my life.
I can't be the forgotten
dream of a self appointed
visionary who needed
to rape to feel inside.

A victim's right is to keep spitting alive.
I may be splitting internal but my bones
are still rigid. Defined not by my trauma
or the bed that they made, I have to
stand tall, to step deep into the tide.

Their ghost is gone.
I'm the one haunting.
I'm the one who walks the dark,
my wail this nightly typing.
Cause it ain't a pipe dream
that I've got the drive to slice lean.
Chopping that fat as I attack

every last act to the satisfact'
of the fat cats and the ghouls
beyond me. I want the mausoleum.
I want a stone bond that'll reach
up and give a reason to keep living.

The grind is clear.
Close eyes to fear.
Bleed long for dear.
My swan song ain't near.

"My Wail"

Accomplishments linger
while I lament what's lost.
Gains came with steep cost.
Brain reconvening my faults
to discuss the third option.

Not defined by the drip.
Won't let my convict' slip.
Not for tears of legacy blown,
but to scoop up that wreck
wrought by bio bonds. I
can't let their sage advice
take center stage in my life.
Can't be the forgotten dream
of an aggrandized visionary
who raped a child trusting.

My victim's right to keep spitting live,
worn by my splitting internal, won't wore
These bones stay rigid, keeping up four walls.
Defined not by trauma or the bed they made,
I stay breathing, so I can stand and step deep
past the land. If I can grit teeth, make waves
I won't be a hollared cannonball into kiddie,
but a swimmer diving for a crowd roaring pretty.

Their ghost is gone. I'm the one haunting.
I'm the one who walks the dark, my wail
this nightly typing. Cause it ain't a pipe
dream that I've got the drive to slice lean.
Chopping that fat as I attack every last act
to the satisfact' of the fat cats and the ghouls
beyond me. I want my mausoleum scene.
I want a stone bond that'll reach eternal
and defend the suffer of erosive masonry.

I want to be a song in the fog of this prison.
I envision a world where my dropped lyrics
are a stellar reprieve told from stories
that launch brand new, old, but this narrative
I gleam is a worm on a demon's string.

I chomp long,
chewing on
as I take my next bite.
Swallow down the tallow,
along with the grin long
on Mephistopheles's chin.
That silver line scraping
my charred barrel. The tar
I seal my inner cracks with,
coming off to let terrible win.
And I could laugh wicked
as drops of praise make me vulnerable,
to a single kick hitting like a brick
as a swing on my own gallow.

I got a long list of grievances
and twenty-five books behind me.
Let the words of art die. Live.
Reject Plan B. Liberty is the lie
that props up a tyrant. Make
a million in Amazon; add
weight to the crusher. Small
press gives them money regardless.
The monopoly takes their fee
no matter what I carve though.

I said I was a butcher,
but they're packaging
soylent green. I'm eating
and "God, that's good!"
At least I got meat for pies.

This heresy of artistry
is making cash for blind views.
They drool for cheap crap
cause it churns ads through.
And the best my blade can sever
is the devil's silver line that I chew.

My art might be a glimmer
in this sunless life, but simmer.
Let the boil congeal to fate.
It's past time this writ lie
stops chopping to waste page.
Trees gonna clap to silence.
That's the audience I leave anyway.

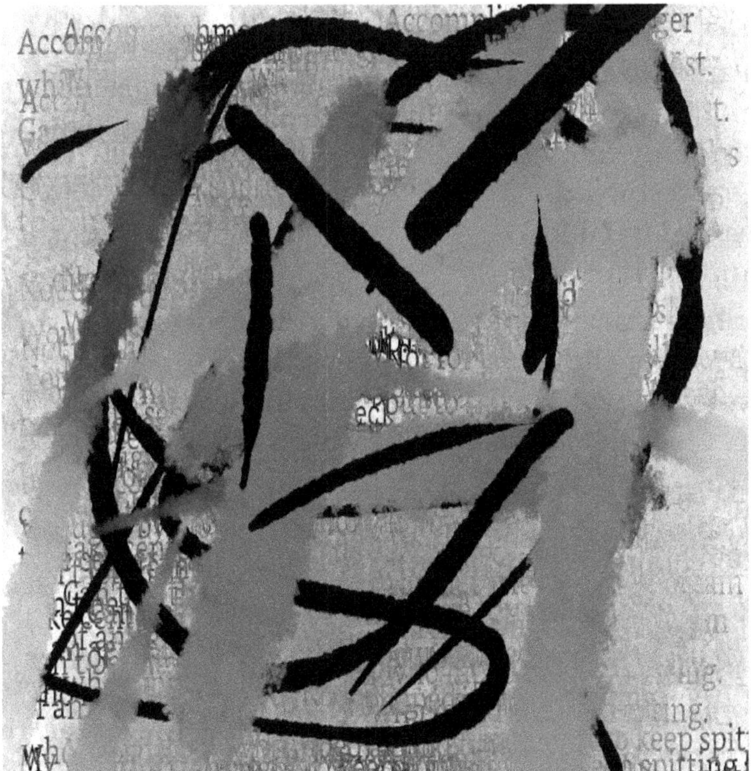

"On the Devil's Line"

Accomplishments lost.
Gains a steep cost.
My faults discuss
the third option.

I won't be a wreck wrung into a sham sage's sling.
Splitting insides tied abound my convict' manifest.
Haunted nightly by my ache to die for medusa's camera.
Basking in that flash, I eat a worm on demon string.
Chewing down tallow 'til drops of praise make my gallow.
My works are nothing more than compiled data files.

Close eyes to fear.
My swan song ain't near.
I'm not collapsed.
Work my station.
Be a cog.
Flee the nation.
Grievances long.
Twenty years of art
left to rot my ego.
Our greatest words
of inspired freedom
prop up a tyrant.

Their heretical art makes cash with blind views.
Pigs drool for cheap crap churning ads.
Best my blade can sever is the devil's line I chew
before the fisher reels in my breathless fat.

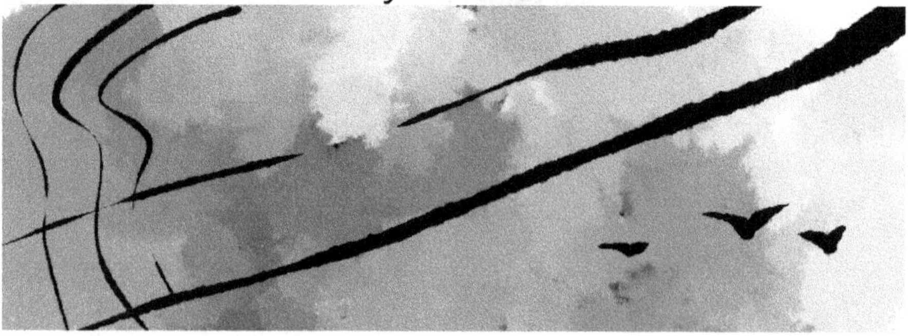

"Passing Accomplishments"

What hope do I have to reach minds
when commerce thrives on content
designed to play ads on phones
that no one cares enough to watch?

An adult life--
a consciousness
--invested to art,
feels wasted. When
I create for blindness.
When success means
bolstering villains.

My best hope lies in defeat,
where I can walk away
from this trap of chewing
on the silver promises
laid with devil's bait.

The promise to die
immortalized in stone
in data propping up
the foundations of tomorrow.

Yet should I die now
my life's fail will be
another tale of victimhood
split so far from the hurt;
no justice can be served.

My every accomplishment
nothing more than
a reminder of what is lost.

..

This ends my dissection of "Untitled Part 113" and with it the end of the Dissection as a whole.

From my end the changes from version to version feel transparent, so obvious that they need not be explained at all, but I know that the distance between my mind and a reader's is so much greater than pages of text can ever bridge. Thus, like the failed academic I am, I invite my readers to look to the remaining poems, and to all poems, and turn their critical eye upon it with skepticism. I invite the aspiring poet to study the meter, the accents, the stanza length, and word choice, and hinted meaning so that they can see what was effective for them as a reader, where I fail, what techniques they might be able to adopt, or adapt, or abandon in their pursuit of artistic truth.

I don't know how much any of this was helpful to a poet looking to improve, to a reader looking for meaning, to a human trying to find that vital break out of plodding disappointment. I could only try and endeavor to be my best, to create with that honesty I have admired in other, and play with art like a child throwing a tantrum in the dictionary.

Thank you all for taking the time to experience my work and thank you all for the inspiration.

"Destiny Diverted"

My death wasn't a question
but a comma in another's day.
A stamp of rage,
accented by my lifeless
body crumpling hip first
into a car's bumper,
while the driver
grips the steering wheel.

Anger baring teeth,
before ape unity
sheds tears
but fails to ease
his brows
as he drives away,
leaving my corpse
bleeding
on the asphalt.

My fault?
My existence.
My walk
reminiscent
of a soldier,
the assassin

viewed past passive
as a cat fleeing a pickle,
a bird alarm for a plane.

His pain?
My gall,
to walk instead of crawl
before his path, as work
sped his heart to expel
all errant ape commune
to make his blood machine
a prelude to my exhumed

self,

rotting past my shelf life.
Suicidal fantasies hampered
not by bliss
but the ending earned denying
the law of Missing Persons.

Hence, I became a nobody.
A lost broken body
drowning in a pool.
I would smile irony,
Morrissey and Morissette
knowing I was a fool
finally becoming
nothing in particular.

Yet my life's path
strayed perpendicular,
rising from death's letter,
seizing a life better
than I have any right
to live and this sight

I'd have given anything
to visit has become

an exquisite corpse
of depressed dreams
on endless stream.
My course only wobbled
by a survivor's wallow
that robs the deep relief
every morn's heave ought
to believe.

For my life is not
the speedbump
of an overworked stiff.
No tragedy of office grift
but a stochastic aberration
in a snake-oil nation ignited

through delighted embrace.
A warm past blaze, deep
and purest synergy.
That ever spoken mystery
was the same unique
divergence that granted
my life a chance undeserving.

T'was love that gave
my life's path a curve.

www.ingramcontent.com/pod-product-compliance
Lightning Source LLC
Chambersburg PA
CBHW071109160426
43196CB00013B/2519
* 9 7 8 1 9 6 9 2 3 9 0 2 1 *